You
Will
Know
The
Truth

You Will Know The Truth

Tabitha Sabou

Acknowledgments

In one way or another, my family has shaped me to some degree. In doing so, they have contributed to the writing of this book. A heartfelt thank you…

To my God, who through His grace and mercy, didn't allow for me to live a mediocre Christian life but instead brought me back to life. With this new life, I pray God will use me to bring many people into His kingdom.

To my husband, Ovi, my partner and best friend, for being the first man to capture my heart and show me true love—for many adventures, hopes, and dreams yet to be fulfilled.

To my children—Ezra (ten), Alec (seven), Iris (six), Clara (five), and John (six months)—my best friends, precious gifts from God. You are etched in my soul, and you have helped me write this book by having a huge part in me being continually shaped into the likeness and image of God.

To my dad, for exhibiting fear and reverence for the Lord and demonstrating with actions what it means to daily seek God in prayer and in reading the scriptures.

To my mom, for being the heart of our family—with big, warm hugs and a huge love for her husband and her children, for instructing me to fight when faced with fear and anxiety, for teaching us all how to be selfless through her actions each and every day.

To my grandma, the American girl, through whom US citizenship was made attainable for our family, allowing my parents to raise their family in this great country of freedom—free to worship God, free to be whatever you desire. *Bunica* taught us all how to be tough.

To my siblings (one sister and four brothers), my best friends growing up. We always had each other—to play with, to laugh with, and to make wonderful memories together. You were my childhood, and I'm thankful for each one of you. My sister Nicoleta, for being my big sister—a pillar of strength in my life, for a close friendship from childhood, for opening my heart to spiritual gifts. And my four brothers: Florin, Danny, David, and Josh—who taught me how to throw a football and taught me that boys are very different from girls, for each one of you making your personal relationship with the Lord your top priority.

I love each one of you and your families dearly. I am blessed to have you in my life.

Contents

Preface

You Will Know The Truth contains biblical truths that will change the way you think and add peace, joy, and contentment to your home. The main scope of this book is to bring unity to the faith by providing clarity on foundational Christian principles, for followers of Christ and for those who are seeking to find truth. Additionally, this book was written to equip and activate Christians to share Jesus with their neighbor, and proclaim Christ to the ends of the earth. Understanding the Holy Spirit and utilizing His gifts is essential in doing so, and in accomplishing God's will on the earth. Proven by God's Word and personal experiences, God's Word applied produces positive results in your life. There are many opinions, but only one truth, and only *the truth applied* will provide real results.

Once the Word reaches the entire globe, the end will come, and Jesus will come back for His own. We must prepare the way for the Lord's return, making crooked paths straight, clearing away confusion by proclaiming the truth. God is real, God is love, and He will save anyone who believes in His Son Jesus. The responsibility of Christians is to spread this good news!

Before I could bring anything of substantial value to others, God had to do a work in me first. I recall praying a simple prayer one day as I was walking in my home; "Lord, show me truth." With so much deception and falsehood surrounding us like never before, my heart was yearning for truth. God honored that simple prayer and began to show me truth about myself, truth about my family, and truth from His Word.

One of the first signs I received from God, that He was bringing me into a new season, was through a bird. I woke up one morning, about four years ago, to the pecking of a lively red cardinal bird. This special family friend of ours pecked at our bedroom window just after 7:00 a.m. daily for the next couple years. It still remains on our property to this day. The first time I laid eyes on this bird, I was in a fog of stress called my life. The pressure from the daily responsibilities of taking care of four young children was heavy. Cooking, cleaning, and picking up Legos was an exhausting routine occurrence. All I was seeing and hearing were the storms in my life. I needed someone to speak peace.

By God's grace, I have been a Christian most of my life—I had some backslidden years in there too. And yet I did not feel the peace and presence of God. I believe God sent this red cardinal and his female counterpart to remind me that He sees me, He knows me, He will never leave me nor forsake me, and that He had a plan for me.

According to Reference.com, "The red cardinal has many symbolic meanings to people of different cultures and faiths. In Christianity, for example, it may represent the fire and vitality of the Holy Spirit as well as the blood of Christ. It can also represent hope and restoration, providing people who are down on their luck motivation so that they don't give up hope. Despite these beliefs, cardinals aren't mentioned in the Christian Bible."

For me, this cardinal reminded me that the Holy Spirit is the comforter, and although He was suppressed, the Spirit was still present in my life. I needed to hear that just like dry land craves fresh living water. Paul says in 1 Thessalonians 5:19, "Do not quench the Spirit," and in Ephesians 4:30 he says, "And do not grieve the Holy Spirit of God, with whom you were sealed for the day of redemption." You do not have to sin in a big way to quench or grieve the Holy Spirit. Being too busy, stressed, or over-worked will do it too, leaving little to no room for the presence of the Holy Spirit in your life.

I was nineteen years old when Jesus baptized me with the Holy Spirit on March 10, 1998. Those were the days of in-home prayer meetings—days of fervent prayer and God always showed up! There are two prophecies I remember vividly. First, that God would use me to take care of the poor and the orphans. Secondly, that God had a big gift for me, spiritual gift that is. Since those days, I have been open and available to God—to work as He sees fit in my life. The stress of life surely can deter us, and other earthly things can temporarily take our eyes off of the goal—to die to self and allow God to live through us by His Holy Spirit. However, God is faithful, and He will finish the work He started in you and in me.

Some time between when I prayed that simple prayer for God to reveal truth, and the red cardinal showing up pecking daily at our window, I received a text message at five o'clock one morning from my brother David.

I was nine years old when David was born. His tiny little blue fingertips captured my heart from the beginning. With my parents working, it was my sister's responsibility and mine to watch over David after school. I was glad to help. We became best buddies. When David was young, under two years old, while trying to look out the window, he fell off my bed, landed on his head, and was in a severe coma. The doctors said if the brain swelling didn't subside they would have to operate on his cranium. The first time that I remember really praying for God to move was then. My parents were at the hospital, and the rest of my siblings were in the living room. I went into the bathroom and shut the door, and in the dark I kneeled and prayed next to the toilet. I prayed that God would stop the swelling. I didn't want the doctors to operate on my baby brother's head. God answered my prayer, my parents' prayers, and the prayers of other Christian family and friends. David recovered nicely. I remember going to physical therapy with him and my mom at Children's Hospital in Detroit. Those experiences led me to choose physical therapy as my answer to, "What do you want to be when you grow up?" I wanted to be a physical therapist to help people.

So I saw and read David's text message later that cold, rainy October morning. David had a dream that I had passed away somehow—maybe a car accident. He immediately prayed for God to intervene, for nothing bad to happen to me. I thanked him then and I thanked David again recently for being conscientious and obedient to the prompting of the Holy Spirit—interceding on my behalf. Whether this dream was literal, symbolic, or just a dream—the truth is, inside I felt like I was dying. Emotionally and physically, I was stressed and felt stretched thin. This was also affecting my spiritual life. I was afraid to die. I was not ready to meet my maker. My kids then were about seven months, two years, three years, and six years old. Dying meant not being there for my kids. I worried that my spot as a wife and mother could easily be replaced by another woman.

Looking back, these are the two things that shaped my identity and gave my life value—being a wife and being a mother. They were my idols, and I didn't even know it. I couldn't imagine what would happen if these two roles were taken from me. They, in essence, were my foundation.

"What's wrong with that?" you may be thinking. Well, God teaches us to have no idols, that He must be number one in our lives. He must be our rock. God is solid and unshakeable. When God is your rock, you can operate in maximum strength—physically, spiritually, mentally, emotionally, and financially. To be able to stand in the day of trial and testing, God must be your rock.

There are many trials and painful experiences we face in life. There will be personal experiences that will cause us to fall, and falls that we must rise up from, take another step, one foot in front of the other—growing stronger with each step. Trials will come. Don't be surprised—be ready. Jesus says, "I have told you these things, so that in me you may have peace. In this world you will have trouble. But take heart! I have overcome the world" (John 16:33). Each experience can mark us for life or can be an opportunity for us to reflect, to correct, and to grow.

Author Anne Ortlund puts it this way; "Pain is God's beautiful gift to make us to lean harder on Him, when He knows we need it." Human beings are selfish by nature, and unfortunately, it takes hardship to get our attention many times. When things are going well, or we think things are going well, we enjoy life and live for the moment oftentimes—a rather superficial way of living. However, when pain happens, the pain goes deep. It is not superficial at all.

Pain must be dealt with, and not kept buried in that deep secret place. If we allow ourselves to be processed or taught by the Holy Spirit, we will have a better character, a deeper sense of what truly is important in life, and a redirected purpose in this journey called life, as a result of our pain. *There is purpose for your pain.*

The most painful life experiences I imagine are loss of a child, passing of a spouse, loss of a parent, or death of a marriage. Although, there are numerous challenges one can face in a lifetime like physical illness, financial distress, or conflict in relationships—that cause disappointment, discouragement, and sorrow.

When faced with any such tragedy or trial, you can respond in different ways. You can blame God, you can blame others, or you can reflect and accept that God sees all things and ultimately is in control of all things. God's Word says, "And we know that God causes everything to work together for the good of those who love God and are called according to his purpose for them" (Romans 8:28). This passage can be hard to accept when you are hurting. However, we can ask God to show us the good He is working. How wonderful that you can pray to the Father and receive answers and comfort by the Holy Spirit, no matter what kind of situation you are walking through!

I believe everything happens for a reason—nothing is by chance or accident. Have you ever prayed for a loved one who was terminally ill to be healed? Have you prayed and believed and yet the Lord still took him or her home? Even in this, God is sovereign. The fact that your loved one passed does not mean that the people praying lacked faith, or that God's power couldn't heal. God has the power to heal instantly.

Perhaps we should be asking the question, "Lord, what is your will in this situation?" God is faithful and will reveal His will. Then you can come into agreement by praying His will for the situation.

Furthermore, some preachers have taught Christians to command or demand God to do X, Y, and Z. This is false teaching. Who's Lord here? He is. Therefore, we ask by faith, in Jesus' name, knowing that God is listening—always taking into account His will (not just holding tight to my own will).

I learned recently that God's will includes *God's timing*. Solomon says in Ecclesiastes, "For everything there is a season…a time to be born and a time to die." Dying is the last stage of living. How we finish the race is what's important. Paul says in Philippians 1:20–21, "In nothing I shall be ashamed, but with all boldness, as always, so now also Christ will be magnified in my body, whether by life or by death. For to me, to live is Christ, and to die is gain." Yes, according to kingdom principles, to die is gain, for those who are rooted in Christ!

Many times we ask God to pull us out of life struggles and to remove the pain we are experiencing. Apostle Paul had a thorn in his side and asked the Lord to remove it three times. We see in 2 Corinthians 12:7–10, Paul writing, "Therefore, in order to keep me from becoming conceited, I was given a thorn in my flesh, a messenger of Satan, to torment me. Three times I pleaded with the Lord to take it away from me. But he said to me, "My grace is sufficient for you, for my power is made perfect in weakness." Therefore I will boast all the more gladly about my weaknesses, so that Christ's power may rest on me. That is why, for Christ's sake, I delight in weaknesses, in insults, in hardships, in persecutions, in difficulties. For when I am weak, then I am strong."

Certainly we *can* ask God to remove us out of a painful situation. However, what I believe we *should* be saying in times of pain, trial, testing, or sorrow is, "Not my will, but yours be done." This is what Jesus did when He was faced with the cross. The pain and suffering He carried was greater than anything we will ever face. Jesus asked the Father to take away the cup of suffering (if He is willing), but ultimately Jesus asked for the Father's will, not His own, to be done.

Apostle Peter writes, as he approaches the conclusion of his first epistle; "But may the God of all grace, who called us to His eternal glory by Christ Jesus, after you have suffered a while, perfect, establish, strengthen, and settle you." *There is purpose for your pain,* and that purpose is to perfect you, to establish you, to strengthen you, and to settle you. Then God can use you for every good work.

9

The work that God called me to, in part, is to share biblical truths with others—in a purposeful, personal, and understandable way. Before this could happen, I had to relinquish control. Part of allowing God to be the rock in my life was giving up control. In human wisdom, having control of something or someone, for example your spouse or children, brings strength and security. However, this human wisdom is severely flawed. We are *seemingly* controlling what we can see with our human eyes. However, what about those things we aren't even aware of? Our view is partial and limited, while the Holy Spirit's perspective is all-encompassing. *God's visibility penetrates all the way to the heart and intent of man.*

God's wisdom says when we are weak—vulnerable, do not have all the answers, yet seek the Lord for truth, and wait on the Holy Spirit to work—we are truly strong. The control has to voluntarily be given back to God. When the Holy Spirit is in the driver's seat of your life, He will lead you to green pastures and still waters (Psalm 23), and you will lack no good thing.

If you are in the driver's seat, I think you will do the best you can. *Your best* will take you only so far and you may get burned out in the process. *Your best* will also make many mistakes.

God in the driver's seat means He leads, you follow, and your life and the lives of those around you will be blessed, even in trials, all the way across the finish line. You know God is leading when your heart can confidently express, "His yoke is easy and His burden is light."

Once this happened for me, I literally felt set free, like someone who was released from prison unexpectedly. I had carried the burden of control since childhood—with insecurities and anxieties all mixed in there. Now I felt so much joy and had true strength. God's Word actually says, "For the joy of the Lord is your strength" (Nehemiah 8:10). This is how I felt.

I wanted to share this joy and the truth of Christ with everyone, literally everyone. If I went to get a pedicure, I made the girl next to me my best friend and looked for ways to comfortably bring Jesus into the conversation. If I was at the bank, I would ask the bank teller if she wanted me to pray for anything specific for her life.

One of my favorite experiences is a Sunday family lunch we had at Wendy's. Having young children and in efforts to minimize stress, oftentimes we would go through the drive-thru and eat in the car. As we were getting our food at the drive-thru window, I noticed a man inside. I didn't know him, however he seemed familiar somehow. We parked to eat and discovered there was a mix-up with our drinks and I ran inside to make the exchange. I noticed the same man with his wife, sitting and eating together at a table, as I walked up to the counter. As I was leaving, I felt prompted to stop at their table.

I didn't know why, but I stopped anyways, and said, "I am a Christian. Is there anything you would like prayer for?" Immediately the man shook his head no. But his wife said, "Actually, we have been trying to have children for some time." I knew exactly how to pray, for my husband and I also struggled and didn't have our first child until after ten years of marriage. I placed my hands on each of their shoulders, bowed my head, and prayed a simple short prayer for God to work in their lives. I then exited with, "Enjoy your meal and have a great day!"

The joy of the Lord also placed messages and truths from God's Word on my heart. I believe that flesh and blood did not reveal these truths, but the Spirit of God did (Matthew 16:17). I had so many thoughts and questions about scriptures I had read over the years. God's Word that was sown in my heart over the past twenty years was popping up in my spirit—coming alive like never before.

One of the first scriptures I meditated on was in John 1, about John the Baptist and his mission to prepare the way for the Lord; "Now this was John's testimony when the Jewish leaders in Jerusalem sent priests and Levites to ask him who he was. He did not fail to confess, but confessed freely, "I am not the Messiah." They asked him, "Then who are you? Are you Elijah?" He said, "I am not." "Are you the Prophet?" He answered, "No." Finally they said, "Who are you? Give us an answer to take back to those who sent us. What do you say about yourself?" John replied in the words of Isaiah the prophet, "I am the voice of one calling in the wilderness, 'Make straight the way for the Lord'" (John 1:19–23). As I was embarking on this new season in my life, I felt very much like John the Baptist felt—the need to make crooked paths straight and make a way for the Lord's *second* coming.

I also came to understand the heart of God like never before, as did Apostle John, the disciple whom Jesus loved. Daily I shared with my husband all of this excitement, joy, and curiosity about the Bible. Finally, Ovi says, "You should write a book."

I began writing ideas on paper, instead of overwhelming him with all of my eagerness. Interestingly enough, I loved to study and read, and in third or fourth grade, I was part of a newly formed club, The Young Author's Club. I agreed with my husband that writing was something that was in my heart, in a deep hidden place. God used my husband to bring it to the forefront of my life. Sometimes, we can't see ourselves. We truly need each other to become better, to stir up the gifts within us, and to develop and grow into full maturity. This is God's will for each Christian.

Our life experiences—how others have treated us, how failures and successes have impacted us, what others have falsely taught us, how fear has controlled us—all such things can be "a plank in our eye." The plank must be removed *or* we must be healed of our past. Then we will be able to provide useful advice to others (Matthew 7: 3-5).

Furthermore, if you do not address your fears properly, they will linger and affect the way you respond to your spouse, your children, parents, friends, church family, and coworkers. It will be the filter that people's words and actions pass through.

Whenever we look through the lens of love coupled with truth, we will always see accurately and interpret accurately. Let God touch your inner person, the real you—making you whole. This can only be done by the working of the Holy Spirit. The Holy Spirit shows us truth in ourselves. When He does, repent, and ask God to correct your vision so you can see and judge clearly, and effectively help others.

Before Jesus comes back for His Church, there is work to be done—crooked paths that need straightening, truths that must be shared, and lives to be reached for His kingdom and for His glory! The next twelve chapters are designed to:

- ❖ Bring unity to the faith, becoming one body of Christ—not a fragmented body

- ❖ Build up the body of Christ, reaching full maturity in Christ

❖ Encourage Christians to love God, through the knowledge and obedience of His commands

❖ Equip and activate Christians to share Jesus with their neighbor, proclaiming Christ to the ends of the earth

❖ Embolden Christians *to know* the Holy Spirit and utilize His gifts—without which we cannot accomplish God's will on the earth

Are you ready to uncover some crucial truths? If you will know the truth—recognize, perceive, understand, and discern the truth—the truth will set you free!

Chapter 1

God Is Real and God Is Love

"In the beginning God created the heavens and the earth. Now the earth was formless and empty, darkness was over the surface of the deep, and the Spirit of God was hovering over the waters" (Genesis 1:1–2). Genesis chapter one continues and describes what God spoke into existence. How awesome that God merely *spoke,* and things were created—the sun, the moon, the stars, galaxies, plants, sea life, animals, and humans to name a few. Although we cannot see God with our human eyes, we surely can see and admire His creation.

We also can't see the Holy Spirit, yet He existed from the beginning, hovering over the waters. However, the portion of the Trinity (God the Father, God the Son, God the Holy Spirit) that *was seen* by the human eye is Jesus Christ, the Son of God. John 1:1–5, 14 says:

In the beginning was the Word, and the Word was with God, and the Word was God. He was in the beginning with God. All things were made through Him, and without Him nothing was made that was made. In Him was life, and the life was the light of men. And the light shines in the darkness, and the darkness did not comprehend it... And the Word became flesh and dwelt among us, and we beheld His glory as of the only begotten of the Father, full of grace and truth.

The Word was with God, the Word was God, and the Word became flesh and dwelt among us. This *flesh* is Jesus Christ, the only Son of God.

There was a point in America when children, adolescents, and adults were very aware and respectful of the existence of God. Children were brought to church and taught in Sunday School that God is the beginning of all things, creator of all things—seen and unseen—and He holds the universe together with His spoken word. Americans believed that God is the most majestic and the most powerful entity—and that He is worthy to receive all glory, all honor, and all praise!

George Washington, the father of this great free nation, once said the following, "It is impossible to govern the world without God. It is the duty of all nations to acknowledge the Providence of Almighty God, to obey his will, to be grateful for his benefits and humbly implore his protection and favor."

As decades passed, the silence and negligence of Christians has allowed for God to be taken out of public schools, courthouses, politics, science, medicine, and most media. Christians should have been standing for truth, even if that meant making people feel uncomfortable at times. As Christians, we have the responsibility to pray, and *also* the responsibility to speak up, take action— defending God given rights and defending truth and justice.

Jesus did just this. He defended God's temple. Matthew 21:12–13 says, "Jesus entered the temple courts and drove out all who were buying and selling there. He overturned the tables of the money changers and the benches of those selling doves. "It is written," he said to them, "My house will be called a house of prayer, but you are making it a den of robbers."

When a person or entity makes decisions that violate God's laws and biblical principles, we have a responsibility to stand for truth and not be silent. Why? We are Christ's representation on this planet. If we do not speak up, who will? People can change, only *after* they are confronted with truth.

And oftentimes, change occurs only *after* they have paid with their wallet or *after* they have received some sort of consequence.

These actions (standing for truth, not remaining silent) are not retaliations; rather, they are actions to bring those responsible to justice. A line of defense against unjust conduct is a line of defense for the ones who received injustice— a wall that speaks on behalf of the mistreated, abused, and even those killed without cause. Justice is not seeking revenge, rather justice is standing for truth and knowing that vengeance is coming and vengeance belongs to the Lord. Romans 12:17–19 says:

> Repay no one evil for evil, but give thought to do what is honorable in the sight of all. If possible, so far as it depends on you, live peaceably with all. Beloved, never avenge yourselves, but leave it to the wrath of God, for it is written, "Vengeance is mine, I will repay," says the Lord.

Being neutral, complacent, and letting an even potentially *bad guy* go, is not godly. However, seeking for the truth of the matter, and holding people or entities accountable for their unjust conduct is godly—doing so in a peaceful and lawful way. Once you have done your part—stand for truth and justice, while never returning evil for evil—God will do the rest, for vengeance belongs to the Lord.

Today, we have a *huge* problem. Some do not believe that God exists. Others believe that He exists, yet they do not have an intimate relationship with their Creator. Approximately 80 percent of Americans believe in the existence of a god, not necessarily the God of the Bible. I believe each person sees God differently, based on their life experiences and how God was presented or represented to them.

The truth is, God is real *and* God is love. The very existence of God and the depth of God's love can be seen not only through creation, but also through the love humans show one to another—husband to wife, mother to her children, one good friend to another, for "God is love" (1 John 4:8). Whenever and wherever love, not lust or any selfish act, is present—God's character is revealed in truth. Apostle Paul defines love so perfectly in 1 Corinthians 13:4–8:

> Love is patient, love is kind. It does not envy, it does not boast, it is not proud. It does not dishonor others, it is not self-seeking, it is not easily angered, it keeps no record of wrongs. Love does not delight in evil but rejoices with the truth. It always protects, always trusts, always

hopes, always perseveres. Love never fails. But where there are prophecies, they will cease; where there are tongues, they will be stilled; where there is knowledge, it will pass away.

Love never fails and love lasts forever. After a person becomes a believer in Christ, their love should grow *past* just loving those close to them, and now loving all people, and seeking to save as many people as possible. Customarily, people love their family members and think this is a very noble act. Loving your family is wonderful and a good start to love. However, love must grow. Loving all humanity is being godly and the essence of Christianity—this is God's heart, as we see in John 3:16; "For God so loved the world that He gave His only begotten Son, that whoever believes in Him should not perish but have everlasting life". Love for all people means sharing Jesus with your neighbor. People have the opportunity to believe, only *after* they hear the message of Jesus.

Since the beginning, God's love has been taken advantage of by mankind. Adam and Eve had it all—the best foods, the best scenery, the best jobs, and the best company (fellowship with the Father). Yet, they risked it all. Through their disobedience, they sinned, severing their relationship with the

Father. The sin automatically separated them and us from God. God is holy, and He cannot tolerate sin.

The only way to restore our relationship with the Father was through the love shown on the cross. Jesus Christ sacrificing His life paved a pathway for salvation, by satisfying the wrath of God toward the sin of humanity. God's love was shown in the *hugest* way possible. The Word says, "In this the love of God was manifest toward us, that God has sent His only begotten Son into the world, that we might live through Him. In this is love, not that we loved God, but that He loved us and sent His Son to be the propitiation for our sins. Beloved, if God so loved us, we also ought to love one another" (1 John 4:9–11).

As a parent, can you imagine sending your only child to a foreign place alone? How about a foreign, imperfect, dirty, and evil place? God removed His perfect Son, from a perfect heaven, and sent Him to us—to show us the way to heaven. God loves us that much!

Unfortunately, Christians, Christ's representatives on earth, oftentimes miss the mark by not truly understanding God's heart. The Holy Spirit—through reading the Bible, praying, and seeking the truth—will teach you about God's heart. The *misrepresentation* of God to family, to church members, and to the world around us, is not only a big deal—it saddens the heart of God. The world will only know the God that we show them—

through our speech, through our works or actions, *through our love*. We are called to love and pray for all mankind—regardless of race, religion, social status, political views, or any other differences we might have.

If we pass the love test, we are right where we should be, as we read in 1 John 4:12–16: "No one has seen God at any time. If we love one another, God abides in us, and His love has been perfected in us. By this we know that we abide in Him, and He in us, because he has given us of His Spirit. And we have seen and testify that the Father has sent the Son as Savior of the world. Whoever confesses that Jesus is the Son of God, God abides in him, and he in God. And we have known and believed the love that God has for us. God is love, and he who abides in love abides in God, and God in him."

Some may have a difficult time accepting God's tremendous love, thinking or being taught that God is a mean God—just waiting to strike people down. This thinking is false. God is love, God is good, and God is also just. One cannot mistake justice for meanness. When we break the law, when we sin, we merely reap the results of what we've done. We must own up to our actions, place responsibility on the appropriate person—ourselves. It is unfair and unjust to blame God for our mistakes or poor actions. However, even when we make mistakes, even when we are living outside of God's will, God's love reaches out—looking to restore, correct, and save.

23

A great example of God's goodness is found in the story of *Jonah*. God spoke to Jonah and sent him on a mission to tell the people of Nineveh, whose wickedness had come up before Him, they had forty days to repent, or else He would judge them. After Jonah ran away from God, and God spoke the second time, Jonah finally listened to God and warned the 120,000 people living in Nineveh. And the people listened; "So the people of Nineveh believed God, proclaimed a fast, and put on sackcloth, from the greatest to the least of them" (Jonah 3:5). *And God changed His mind;* "Then God saw their works, that they turned from their evil way; and God relented from the disaster that He had said He would bring upon them, and He did not do it" (Jonah 3:10). If the heart of God was to simply destroy, He wouldn't have sent Jonah to warn the people of Nineveh *first*, regarding their wickedness, and give them a chance to change.

Interestingly enough, Jonah was *dissatisfied* and even angry with God's decision. In his displeasure, Jonah prays to the Lord and says, "I know that you are a gracious and merciful God, slow to anger and abundant in loving-kindness, One who relents from doing harm" (Jonah 4:2). Pretty much, Jonah is saying, "I told you so... I told you that you were a good God." Yes, God *is* a good God, and desires restoration and salvation for all of His creation. When God's love is perfected in us, we also will have the same desires that the Father has—to seek and save that which is lost.

24

God makes this statement at the end of the book of Jonah; "Should I not pity Nineveh, that great city, in which are more than one hundred and twenty thousand persons who cannot discern between their right hand and their left?" You see, before bringing judgment, God reveals truth to people, allowing them a fair opportunity to repent *or* turn from their evil ways. Aren't you glad that God, not man, is the ultimate judge, and that He judges fairly?

Some people imagine that God is a very busy God. Does He really see me, have time for me, and care about me? The answer to all these questions is *absolutely yes*. To find out the plans He has for you, you must read His Word and spend time with Him in prayer—not because you have to, not to earn your salvation (because you can't)—but because you desire a relationship with the Creator of all things. You don't earn points by singing praise songs, or praying. Rather, the reward is being in His presence!

This is the path to a relationship with the Lord—draw near to Him, and in return He will draw near to you. Who makes the first move? You and I do. We know that the *very first move* was made by God—sending His son Jesus to live as a perfect example, and to die an excruciating death for my sin and your sin. On this path, there are no shortcuts. Faith and patience are crucial ingredients, without which this relationship will not work.

Faith—you must believe that God exists, that His love sent His Son Jesus to pay the ultimate price, and you must surrender to His lordship. Patience—you will inherit the promises of God, in God's timing, if you don't give up. Don't wait to wake up one day super pumped-up about reading the Bible and praying. Do it on purpose. We must put our flesh under submission and not allow it to dictate how we will live our lives and what our day's schedule will look like.

If you count yourself a Christian, you have a responsibility to have the nature of Christ. In Matthew 5: 13–14, Jesus tells His disciples and the multitudes, "You are the salt of the earth… You are the light of the world." What does salt do? Salt adds flavor and preserves. A little salt goes a long way, and too much salt makes a person gag—a wise pastor friend of ours said. Just by stepping into a room, you can change the environment, for the glory of God. But if you remain silent, if you are a *secret Christian*, you become useless for God's kingdom. Speak up, stand for truth, adding much needed flavor to this world, in need of a Savior.

Furthermore, when you turn on a lamp, what happens? It disperses the darkness. But if you place a blanket over the lamp, it is dark again. Christians are meant to shine for all to see. Look and pray for opportunities to be the light. *Here are some of my own experiences of being a practical Christian.*

I worked as a pharmaceutical sales representative for eight years, before being a stay-at-home, and homeschooling mom. During that time, people knew I was a Christian. I didn't hide it, neither did I hide myself from being around my colleagues—I just didn't do all the things that they did. Instead, I was my usual self. I prayed over my meals, acted in a godly fashion to the best of my ability, and when I had the opportunity to share Christ, I did.

I remember winning some sales contest and being asked to write about the following topic: "If you could have dinner with anyone, who would it be?" Wow! What an opportunity. I said if I could have dinner with anyone, I would pick Jesus, and I wrote why. My response was sent not only to my team but to many others in the company. I don't know how many people were impacted by my words. However, one of my Christian colleagues, who I didn't know was a Christian, reached out and commended me for my boldness. Perhaps my words were more of a wake-up call to silent Christians. Nonetheless, it is fun and rewarding to *live out loud* for Christ. As far as I'm concerned, it is the only way to live. Try it and you will see what I mean!

Furthermore, in college I took a psychology class as part of my prerequisite courses. One of the topics was abortion. Long story short, I was the only one in the class that spoke up against abortion—the rest were either vocal about abortion being a choice women should have, or silent. This was the case with many other topics as well. The professor noticed my stance on things, and later in the semester asked me to see him during office hours, so I went. He expressed his appreciation for my fight for what I believe and also said he started going back to church. This professor was probably in his seventies, retired from Ford Motor Company, and took on psychology as a hobby. How awesome that God caused our paths to cross, and hopefully I was a part of his return to the faith.

One day, the entire world will know that God is love through our love (John 13:35), the love of Christians who walk with the Lord daily—the love we show one toward another. When you love your brother, you are showing God's love in the present, right now, active. This type of love and unity will be the catalyst of a revival—a holy movement that will heal the sick and save the lost. The crowds found Jesus, followed Jesus, and listened to His message—highly due to the miracles He performed. The fact that he also fed them miraculous bread and fish was a nice bonus. In the same way, I believe people in the world will find us, Christians. Once we live in truth, walk in love and unity as one body of Christ—miracles and healings will occur as a normal part of the Christian life and church services. It will not be a show, it will be the norm, and God will get all the credit!

I am learning that more than one person is needed to start revival. It is a team effort. "Where two or three are gathered, I am there," says the Lord. It can start with one family, one church body, united in love and truth. From this point, the spread and multiplication can be to the ends of the earth!

In addition to loving our brother, we are called to love all people. It may seem difficult, even impossible, to love all people, especially those who have hurt you. To truly forgive someone from a past hurt—whether the person apologized or not—is a work of the Holy Spirit and can be accomplished. The Bible says to "overcome evil with good" (Romans 12:21), and to "bless those who persecute you and pray for those who despitefully use you" (Luke 6: 27–28). Here is our answer. When anger, hatred, or fear rises up against someone, you bless and pray for that person—instead of getting offended, defensive, or holding hatred toward him or her. I've learned to do this. Once I pray for the person (do it on the spot, even in your mind), peace takes over. It is amazing! And if the person is worthy of blessing, it will remain. And if not, the blessing will return back to you (Mathew 10:13). God is so good and so fair.

In the natural, our flesh or human nature, this type of thing won't just happen one day. We have to make it happen on purpose. Take action! Bless and pray for those around you that you encounter, especially those who have hurt you.

I like to remind myself often of the following truth—I am not perfect and neither are you. We are all broken people, in a broken world, in need of a Savior. Keeping this in mind sets us up for relating to others, feeling compassion for others, praying for others, and loving all people. Then the world will know God is love, because we as Christians are portraying God as being a loving God, through our actions. How else will the world know? It is our responsibility to show Jesus, accurately represented to this world. He's a good God, He's a forgiving God, and His mercies are new every morning!

One of my favorite scriptures is from Romans 8:35–39, written by Apostle Paul, a man that experienced the love of God in an actual encounter on his way to Damascus. Paul, then Saul, did not know Jesus. On the contrary, he was persecuting followers of Christ. However, Paul thought he was doing the will of God. God in His grace and mercy *chose* Paul to be a follower of Jesus, an apostle, and a major contender in the Christian faith. The love Christ showed to Paul was reciprocated and evident through Paul's writings, his leadership, his discipleship, and even through Paul's death: "Based on historical events of the day, it is likely that Paul was beheaded, possibly around the same time that Peter was crucified" (Christianity.com). The love Paul knew personally about Christ reads as follows from Romans 8:

Who shall separate us from the love of Christ? Shall tribulation, or distress, or persecution, or famine, or nakedness, or peril, or sword? As it is written: "For Your sake we are killed all day long; We are accounted as sheep for the slaughter." Yet in all these things we are more than conquerors through Him who loved us. For I am persuaded that neither death nor life, nor angels nor principalities nor powers, nor things present nor things to come, nor height nor depth, nor any other created thing, shall be able to separate us from the love of God which is in Christ Jesus our Lord.

Today we are living in some very uncertain times. From a human standpoint, I can't imagine what the world will look like for our children and grandchildren. However, one thing is certain, one thing can be counted on today and for eternity— the deep, the unbreakable, the eternal love of God! His love will hold us and never forsake us.

Seek the Lord while He may still be found. May you know Him and the power of His resurrection. May you have eternal life found only through Jesus Christ.

Chapter 2

Jesus Is the Only Way to God

If we can agree that there is a higher power, a God in heaven, wouldn't one path to Him be enough? According to Google, there are currently 4,300 religions of the world. That's a large number, and that represents 4,300 different religious paths one can take. Since the beginning, humans have tried to fill the internal void, which God himself put inside of us. King Solomon, the wisest man who ever lived, said about God, "He has made everything beautiful in its time. He has also set eternity in the human heart; yet no one can fathom what God has done from beginning to end" (Ecclesiastes 3:11).

We were designed for fellowship, or friendship, with our God. Ultimately, each person is searching for a higher power, a higher purpose, and to be loved and rescued by a Savior.

The Bible says that we were born in sin (Psalm 51:5). Take a look at any child, as young as six months old or even younger, who will pout, kick and scream, or cry just to get their way—a toy, a different type of food, delay bedtime, extend playtime, etc. We are born selfish and unruly. Being selfish and unruly gets us into trouble and into sin.

Furthermore, there is sin that exists in the human heart: "But each person is tempted when he is lured and enticed by his own desire. Then desire when it has conceived gives birth to sin, and sin when it is fully grown brings forth death" (James 1:14–15). It all starts with a desire, or *the intent of the heart.* That is why we need a new heart, a clean heart, a heart that has God-desires, not my own desires.

Before David sinned with Bathsheba, he saw her *and* desired her in his heart first. Then, because he was king, was able to make his desires a reality, and invited her to his palace to commit adultery with her. Soon after, David also committed murder. He was the reason Bathsheba's husband died in battle.

Thankfully, this is only part of David's story. Although he paid the heavy price of his sin, with the death of his son and other punishments described in 2 Samuel—still, David was a man after God's own heart, for David did whatever God told him to do.

Most of us can recall and admit we have lied, stolen, or cheated at some point in our life. Our sinful nature is very obvious when we try living just one day free from envy, jealousy, strife, or unrighteous anger. It is important to note that unrighteous anger seeks destruction, while *righteous anger*, which is godly anger and without sin, seeks restoration and rehabilitation. Nonetheless, in our flesh or human nature, it is impossible to live without sinning in some way. Christ calls us to take on His nature, thus allowing us to live more and more like Christ, less and less like the world, until we are perfected in Him and sinless. Our behavior doesn't save us—salvation is through Jesus alone. However, our behavior should represent Christ's character and behavior—more and more each day.

So there is no way around this reality; "All have sinned and fall short of the glory of God" (Romans 3:23). All means *all*. For the person who says, "I have done nothing wrong, therefore, why do I need a savior?"—that is his sin, thinking he is self-righteous. Our best deeds are like filthy rags (Isaiah 64:6). To enter heaven, we need new clothes, *white clothes*—clothes only Christ can provide (Revelation 19:8).

Sin is similar to cancer. If it isn't removed, it will lead to death. If cancer was a disease, which it is, wouldn't *one cure* suffice to put an end to this terrible disease? And if the medical community then claimed to find 4,300 cures to cancer, would that even be believable? There is one cure for cancer.

Likewise, there is *one cure* for the sinful human heart that is searching for purpose and unconditional love. Jesus says in John 14:6, "I am the way, the truth, and the life. No one comes to the Father except through me." In other words, Jesus is saying He is the cure, *the only cure*, for the sinful human heart, and the only One who can restore humanity's relationship with the Father. In John 10:9, Jesus says, "I am the gate. If anyone enters through Me, he will be saved. He will come in and go out and find pasture." Jesus speaks of being a gate also in Matthew 7. Jesus describes Himself as being the *narrow gate*, the one gate that leads to life. The wide gate leads to destruction, hence the 4,300 different religions that exist today.

Jesus came to this earth to die. This was His mission, to be crucified. It was the only way to satisfy God's wrath toward sin. Apostle John says in 1 John 2:2, "He [Jesus] is the propitiation for our sins, and not for ours only but also for the sins of the whole world." The precious blood of Jesus paid the price for you, for me. We can only be found perfect once we are covered by the blood of Jesus. Imagine a mama hen sheltering and embracing her little chicks under her wings. This is what Jesus does for us. We must surrender, and we must let Him embrace us. The Lord never uses force. Draw close to Him, if you want to be in God's presence.

35

We hear about people *getting saved.* What exactly does one have to do to be saved? Acts 16:30–31 speaks of the Philippian jailor's conversation with Paul and Silas: "Sir, what must I do to be saved?" Paul and Silas respond, "Believe in the Lord Jesus, and you will be saved, you and your household." Furthermore in Mark, Jesus says, "Whoever believes and is baptized will be saved, but whoever does not believe will be condemned" (Mark 16:16). Jesus also talks about being *born again* in John 3: "Most assuredly, I say to you, unless one is born of water and the Spirit, he cannot enter the kingdom of god. That which is born of the flesh is flesh, and that which is born of the Spirit is spirit."

One day Jesus and His disciples were having a conversation about a rich man getting saved, and that his chances were very slim of receiving salvation. Jesus' disciples were astonished and asked, "Who then can be saved?" Jesus responds, "With men this is impossible, but with God all things are possible" (Matthew 19:26).

To better understand the concept of salvation, one can compare and contrast it with making a transaction. In any major purchase or transaction, there is a special item for sale, a seller, and an interested buyer. Regarding salvation and eternity, you are the special item for sale, and you also are the seller— you decide who the buyer will be. God is an interested buyer, and so is the devil. The devil will try to buy you with momentary worldly pleasures, with lies, and with false promises. However, God is ready to be the highest bidder, pay the highest price. The price paid for you is the blood of Jesus Christ on the cross. There is no greater payment, no greater transaction, than between the sinful human soul and the blood shed at Golgotha. Praise His name forever! Jesus prays the following prayer about Himself, as His time for crucifixion draws near:

> Father, the hour has come. Glorify Your Son, that Your Son also may glorify You, as You have given Him authority over all flesh, that He should give eternal life to as many as You have given Him. And this is eternal life, that they may know You, the only true God, and Jesus Christ whom You have sent. I have glorified You on the earth. I have finished the work which you have given Me to do. And now, O Father, glorify Me together with Yourself, with the glory which I had with You before the world was. (John 17: 1-5)

Once you accept Jesus in your heart as Lord and Savior, you accept the offer—*Lord* meaning Jesus holds the number one place in your heart and *Savior* meaning Jesus saved you from sin and death, giving you life in abundance instead. Accepting the offer means you no longer belong to yourself, or this world, or the devil. You were bought with a price, the highest price. You now belong to God and are part of God's family. You now have God as your Father, Jesus as your brother, and the Holy Spirit beside you and in you—providing guidance, comfort, and protection. Everything God has belongs to you, His child. In order to have constant fellowship with God, abide in Him by obeying His word.

If you don't have Jesus as your Lord and Savior today, be honest about the condition of your heart and invite Jesus in. Begin a relationship with the Father, His Son Jesus, and the Holy Spirit—a relationship that will last an eternity. Talk to God daily (prayer), and read His Word daily. I recommend starting with Matthew and reading the entire New Testament at least a couple of times before moving to the Old Testament. The next day after I got saved, I started to read the Bible. It is what I had seen my Dad do consistently, daily, for years—also coupled with daily prayer. Thankfully, my parents have been good, godly examples of fearing the Lord and incorporating and considering the Lord first and foremost in all areas of life. Being Christian was not just a Sunday thing, but an everyday, lifelong, eternal thing; and it was top priority.

If you are a Christian who feels distant from the Lord, or has lived an average or somewhat boring Christian life, it's time to step it up! Daily reading and studying God's Word is critical. Recently, I started a new practice. I will read a chapter, verse by verse, and write down in my notebook what I just read, verse by verse. This has helped my mind pay better attention to details and grasp more information. Try it yourself!

Daily reading the Bible and daily prayer needs to be a part of your life. Praying is heartfelt issues laid at the feet of Jesus by faith. When you talk to God, know that He is listening and will move on your behalf. Your job, my job, is to have faith and to have patience. James 5:16 says, "...The effective, fervent prayer of a righteous man avails much." *Effective* means successful in producing a desired or intended result, *fervent* means having a passionate intensity (hot, burning, glowing), and *avails* means to produce or result in as a benefit or advantage. My oldest son asked me one day, "Mama, why do you

39

pray so loud sometimes?" I answered in the following manner. When you are sick, downtrodden, hopeless, fearful, and looking for answers—what kind of prayer would you like lifted up on your behalf? This is it, right here—the effective, fervent prayer. This prayer is not just about being loud. It is a powerful prayer inspired and led by the Holy Spirit, and comes from a heart sold out for Jesus.

Most people know that when you pray, you talk to God. However, Jesus tells us how to pray and how *not* to pray. Jesus says not to pray to be seen by others—like trying to impress others in church; and not to use many words or vain repetitions. Rather, Jesus tells us in Matthew 6:6, "But when you pray, go into your room, close the door and pray to your Father, who is unseen. Then your Father, who sees what is done in secret, will reward you openly." Whether during private prayer or during corporate prayer (in church), pray sincerely from the heart.

Jesus gives us the model prayer. Let us now study each part of *The Lord's Prayer*. Together, we will uncover what it means for us right now, and how it should be shaping our thinking and behavior.

The Lord's Prayer

"Our Father who art in heaven"

God is reigning in heaven, and He is our Father! Even the best earthly father falls short, and only our heavenly Father knows the deepest parts of our soul, meets all of our needs, and provides unconditional love and purpose to His children.

"Hallowed be thy name"

Hallowed means *made holy, consecrated*. God is holy, and we must also be holy. This can only be done by the work of the Holy Spirit inside of us, and our voluntary surrender to His leading and instructions each day.

"Thy kingdom come, Thy will be done, on earth as it is in heaven"

We are asking for His kingdom to come; as opposed to having our kingdom, having our rule, having our way. God's will is being done in heaven, a perfect place without sin. God's plan is for His will to be done on earth as well. This part depends on us, His children. When we seek God in prayer, in fasting, and in spending time in His Word, God shows us what His will is. We must *believe* His will, *agree* with His will, and *pray* His will.

And then His will can and will take place in our dimension, or on earth. Before God makes a move on earth, He shares what He will do with His own, by the Holy Spirit. We must slow down, be still, find silence, draw close, get to know the heart of the Father— then we will be able to discern the will of the Father.

"Give us this day our daily bread"

The Bible says, "Man will not live by bread alone, but by every word that proceeds out of the mouth of God" (Matthew 4:4). Therefore, when we pray "give us this day our daily bread," we are asking for food not only for our physical body but also for our spirit. This spiritual food comes from reading God's Word. The Bible's words are food for your soul. Just like we feed our physical bodies with food *daily*, we must feed our spirit with spiritual food or the Word of God *daily*. A goal my family and I have is to read one chapter from God's Word together, out loud, before bedtime each day. Certainly, you can read more. However, a little goes a long way. If you read consistently and if you are attentive and read out loud, you will find that, "faith comes by hearing and hearing from the Word of God." Surely *hearing* the message is a heart issue, however, I find that reading out loud helps in staying focused and on track, and it is a verbal proclamation as well. Words are powerful, especially God's Words expressed out loud.

"And forgive us our trespasses, as we forgive those who trespass against us"

We ask God to forgive us in the same manner that we forgive others who have hurt or wronged us. Matthew 6:14–16 says, "For if you forgive other people when they sin against you, your heavenly Father will also forgive you. But if you do not forgive others their sins, your Father will not forgive your sins." So if we can't forgive someone who has caused us pain or anger, in like manner, God can't forgive us. If we forgive partially, with conditions, again, that gets factored in, and God can't give us total forgiveness, because of our actions of unforgiveness toward others. The Bible *doesn't* say, "Forgive someone if they ask for forgiveness." Regardless of whether a person asks of your forgiveness or not, we *must* forgive so that God can forgive us. This is God's law that we must follow. However, if *you* wronged someone, intentionally or unintentionally, you owe that person an apology. I've had to apologize to my kids, my husband, and others many times—for acting in an ungodly way toward them.

If you have trouble forgiving someone, tell God about it. Ask Him to help you forgive. The Bible says to bless those that persecute you and despitefully use you (Matthew 5:44), and later in the book of Matthew, that if a person isn't worthy of the blessing, the blessing will return back to you (Matthew 10: 13). It is a win-win situation. God is amazing,

43

and His ways are so much higher than the ways of man!

"And lead us not into temptation, but deliver us from evil"

We are asking God not to lead us into temptation. However, if we are tempted, God will be there; "No temptation has overtaken you that is not common to man. God is faithful, and he will not let you be tempted beyond your ability, but with the temptation he will also provide the way of escape, that you may be able to endure it" (1 Corinthians 10:13).

After water baptism and the Holy Spirit descending on Jesus like a dove, Jesus was led by the Holy Spirit into the wilderness to be tempted by the devil (Matthew 4). God allowed the tempting, but the tempting came from the devil (see also James 1:13). It could only come from him, for no evil exist in God. The very definition of tempt is "the desire to do something wrong or unwise." We see the results of the devil's three attempts to tempt Jesus. The devil failed, for no evil existed in Jesus. Jesus passed the test and was ready to begin His public ministry. We are not Jesus—however, the same Holy Spirit lives in Christians (Romans 8:11). And we can ask God to deliver us, or save us, from the devil and his plans. God listens and works in the seen and unseen (or spiritual) realm, on our behalf.

"For thine is the kingdom, and the power, and the glory, for ever and ever"

He is King of kings, Lord of lords! All power is His, in heaven and on earth! All glory, magnificence, and great beauty belongs to God! Hallelujah!

"Amen"

Let it be so! Anytime we say amen, we come into agreement with God's Word or what is being said or preached. This is a powerful thing to practice. If you agree, say amen!

God's Word has much to teach us about praying—for it also teaches us to *pray without ceasing* (1 Thessalonians 5: 17). This may sound impossible. We all have busy lives. Most have to hold down a full-time job, go to school, run a home, operate a business, raise children, or homeschool children. The list is endless. As a busy mother of five, I *now* find myself praying all day long. Being a wife and mother pushes you to a different level, and gladly, one of the skills I acquired is *praying without ceasing*. "Lord, help me. Lord, teach me. Lord, give me strength." Simple prayers from the depth of your being are effective and what God desires from us, all day long, everyday.

The verses before and after *pray without ceasing* are, "Rejoice at all times... Give thanks in every circumstance, for this is God's will for you in Christ Jesus" (1 Thessalonians 5:16–18). Besides praying continually, being thankful and joyful continually—are also crucial elements.

One thing my mom taught me was to pray first thing in the morning, and I have gotten into the habit of saying first thing in the morning, "Thank you, Father, for a new day." I try to start each day with opening my heart to the Lord and thanking Him for another chance to work for Him—even if it is a sentence to start with. Later in the morning time, I pray with and for my kids individually. It doesn't always go as planned. However, this is the goal. The sweetest words come from their heart. The Holy Spirit inside of us teaches us how to pray for ourselves, for our spouse, for our children, our families, church body, for the body of Christ around the globe, for the president and all the world leaders, and for all people to be saved. Jesus prayed, the apostles prayed, and we must also pray.

Fasting & Praying

In addition to praying, the early Church fasted and prayed often (see the book of Acts). The apostles fasted when they were seeking guidance from the Lord, when they were sending disciples out, and when they tried casting out certain demons. When my grandmother got saved, she had a potty-mouth and decided she would not feed her mouth until it submitted itself and stopped swearing.

The Bible says, "Out of the abundance of the heart, the mouth speaks;" and my grandma had the right idea—crucify the flesh, weaken the flesh, so God's glory can fill you. When we are weak, we are strong because the Holy Spirit is able to rise up and fill us. We must purify ourselves of our old nature and "present our bodies as a living sacrifice, holy and acceptable to God, which is our spiritual worship" (Romans 12:1).

Even from personal experience, fasting crucifies the flesh. You are literally depriving it of what it wants, coffee probably more than food, therefore putting it into submission—humbling thyself. The Bible says that the spirit is willing, but the flesh is weak, or the flesh drags us down and keeps us from doing what the spirit wants. So what do we do? We crucify it. When we are humble, the Holy Spirit has room to fill us.

Oftentimes, the Holy Spirit will put someone on my heart to fast for and with. I will reach out and partner together in fasting and prayer for a specific purpose—physical healing, finding God's partner in marriage, financial breakthrough, truth and justice to be served—you name it. When there are no specific needs, I pray and fast for God to continue to keep me humble and use me for His glory.

Every time you fast, you are built in the spirit. I have noticed this certainly. Nothing we do in the Lord's name is in vain. God will reward your fasting and praying. You will grow closer to the Lord, your faith will increase, you will see healings with your own eyes, you will grow in boldness to witness to others, and your family and those around you will also be blessed by what you are doing.

Fasting is a must. Matthew 6:16 says, "And when you fast, don't make it obvious, as the hypocrites do, for they try to look miserable and disheveled so people will admire them for their fasting. I tell you the truth, that is the only reward they will ever get." Jesus says to His disciples *when* you fast, not *if* you fast. Fasting is part of the Christian life— and fasting has rewards.

Challenge yourself to fast one day per week, every week. I have found it easier to fast if I pick the same day each week, like Wednesdays for example, to fast. Your mind and body will adjust to your weekly, consistent commitment. If you haven't fasted for some time, try to fast until noon. Then after a month, try to fast until 3:00 p.m. The Bible isn't specific about the length of the fast. While I was growing up, my parents fasted from midnight the night before until sundown of that following day, having no food or water.

When I fast, I have no coffee and no food, and sometimes I take water if I need it. Jesus didn't eat for forty days and forty nights, and then the Bible says He was hungry. I don't think God expects this of us—unless He tells you to do so by His Holy Spirit. In that case, He will give you the strength to fulfill His command, and you will live through it. One time I fasted until sundown, and it was very difficult for me.

I suggest working your way up to a full day fast. But if you can't, do what you can rather than abandon fasting altogether.

Also, don't feel like you have to read the Bible for hours and pray for hours on the day you fast. God knows the commitments you have (family, work, etc.), and finding pockets of time to pray and read God's Word is sufficient. Probably the best time to do so would be when you would regularly eat your meal—for example lunchtime. Take that time to feed your spirit instead of your belly. Fasting and praying one to two days a week (as the Holy Spirit leads and your health status allows) is a fast, easy way to humble your flesh and feel God's presence again—not to earn salvation or favor, but to draw near to your Father.

I have lived through these circumstances as well as the remedies. When you purposefully draw closer to the Lord, the Lord will draw near to you (James 4:8). God has a plan. The plan is to prosper and not harm, to give you a hope and a future!

Who I Am In Christ

Years ago, my husband and I attended a megachurch, and before they got derailed by constantly teaching the prosperity gospel, there were some very valuable truths we learned from the pastor there—truths that were not usually taught in our traditional home church.

The environment, the church I was raised in, told me through their *actions* that God's love and salvation were based on performance. Even after I was saved at eighteen years old, water baptized that same year, and received the baptism of the Holy Spirit with the evidence of speaking in tongues the following spring, I still doubted my salvation.

Due to my daily actions (doing great one moment, then frustrated or angry the next), I thought I gained and lost my salvation so many times. One Sunday evening at prayer meeting, a prophet spoke to me and said, "Your name is written in the Book of Life." I was blown away by the news and could not stop sobbing!

This experience—well, the Holy Spirit working through my brother in Christ—helped me believe I was truly saved. This example also shows how important spiritual gifts are to teach, to encourage, and to restore. The Holy Spirit exposes lies by presenting truth.

The idea that my relationship with God was based on how much good I did or how much I failed that day was literally engrained in the fabric of my soul. What a big lie! We are made right with God because of Jesus paying the price with His own blood—the blood of the King of kings, the blood of the Lord of lords! Good works flow out of a relationship with Jesus. Good works do not save you or keep you saved. Good works are evidence that you have been saved by Christ. And when we fall, we get back up; "The righteous may fall seven times but still get up…"

(Proverbs 24:16). We get back up and come to Jesus, asking for forgiveness, with repentance, and move forward in His grace.

The late Pastor Jack Wallace taught us who we were in Christ Jesus, constantly and repeatedly, and it stuck. He spoke the following words often:

- ❖ "I am the righteousness of God in Christ Jesus."

- ❖ "I am the head and not the tail, above only and not beneath."

- ❖ "No weapon formed against me shall prosper."

- ❖ "Greater is He that is in me than he that is in the world."

- ❖ "For I know the plans I have for you—plans to prosper you and not harm you, plans to give you a hope and a future."

It is important to know what God says about you and to confess those things out loud until it becomes a part of you. The thoughts of being worthless, inadequate, and a failure—all come from the devil. Just like a good, loving parent encourages his child and doesn't destroy him with diminishing words, how much more our heavenly Father has good thoughts, awesome plans, and words of encouragement for us?

God's Words of encouragement lie in His Word, in the mouth of prophets, and in the body of Christ (church body). He gives gifts to the church body, so that we can help and encourage each other along this journey on earth, ensuring we finish the race strongly (and bring others with us). Paul says in 2 Timothy 4:7–8, "I have fought the good fight, I have finished the race, I have kept the faith. Henceforth there is laid up for me the crown of righteousness, which the Lord, the righteous judge, will award to me on that day, and not only to me but also to all who have loved his appearing."

All of God's promises are yes and amen. God's love is perfect and is not based on our performance, or even our obedience; "While we were yet sinners, Christ showed His love for us by His undeserved, selfless death on the cross" (Romans 5:8). However, God wants you to obey Him in all things. *Obedience* to His Word and the Holy Spirit brings the Lord delight and produces blessings in your life. *Disobedience* causes you to walk around the mountain one more time and stay in the wilderness longer than you have to, as did the children of Israel.

When we disobey, God speaks a word of correction first. If we don't yield to it, He may chastise us. The Bible says, "God chastises those He loves." Until we have breath, His love reaches out. When you sin, run to God, instead of running away from God. He will meet you in your hour of need!

Let's live a life that always says, "Not my will but your will be done." Daily living by faith and not by sight may come with criticisms. Live by faith anyways, and trust God with the unknown. Don't allow yourself to be offended by what others say about you. Remember, the Word says, "If they rejected me, they will reject you." In fact, when others reject the message God puts on your heart to share with others (a message coming out of a heart of love and based on truth), that person is actually rejecting God, so don't get offended. Many of Jesus' family members didn't believe in Jesus until after His resurrection.

The righteous shall live by faith and faith is needed now more than ever. Luke 18:8 says, "When the Son of Man comes, will he find faith on the earth?" As much as it depends on us, let the answer be *yes*.

You belong to God, you are the righteousness of God in Christ Jesus, and you must choose Christ to be your rock; "Therefore thus says the Lord GOD, 'Behold, I am laying in Zion a stone, a tested stone, a costly cornerstone for the foundation, firmly placed. He who believes in it will not be disturbed'" (Isaiah 28:16). Jesus can be trusted to be our firm foundation. No matter how young, how old, how attractive or less attractive you feel, how rich or poor you are, how successful you are in relationships, how you have failed in relationships, regardless of how others treat you and how your *friends* on social media make you feel—Jesus Christ's opinion of you is the same. You are the righteousness of God in Christ Jesus, and He loves you with an eternal love! Nothing can separate you from God's love. Let Jesus be your solid rock and foundation, and nothing will shake you much. The winds will blow, but the storms will not destroy you.

I often will hypothesize *worst-case scenarios*; and on the journey of life, the worst-case scenario is everyone abandons you (or you die). Even if someone were to reach this point, God says, "I will never leave you or forsake you!" This is a solid promise. What more can a person want than to have God by his or her side? And to die means I leave this life and enter into glory! So lay down your burden and relax in the arms of your Father. Family, friends, and a good career are wonderful; but our rock must be Jesus. We are building on the rock, not sand, when we obey the instructions of Jesus (Matthew 7:24).

What Denomination Is the Right Denomination?

I was raised in a Romanian Pentecostal church. However, many of my friends I grew up with or worked with are

Catholic. I have not fully studied the Catholic religion, however, I was pleasantly surprised when I attended my cousin's wedding ceremony—to see that the truth of the Gospel was presented by the priest. It was amazing, refreshing, and relieving. The priest was preaching the Bible.

From what I know, Catholics confess their sins to the priest. The devil wants you to keep things in the dark, and if you obey him, you will remain in the chains of sin. The Bible says, "If we confess our sins, He is faithful and just to forgives us our sins" (1 John 1:9). Confessing sin is crucial in order to receive forgiveness and break the chains of sin and addiction.

So we confess our sins, ask for forgiveness in Jesus' name, and God is the one who grants us forgiveness of sin, not a priest or a man—but God. We confess to man (James 5:16) and receive forgiveness from God.

The only mediator between man and God is Jesus. Any other mediator—the priest, the pope, Virgin Mary, or any other thing—is not biblical. Jesus is our mediator and teaches us how to pray, and that prayer is straight to the Father in heaven. And we pray in Jesus' name—for, He paid the price for our sin, and there is power in the name of Jesus!

In addition to the Pentecostal and Catholic religions, there are numerous Christian religions. Currently 2.42 billion people call themselves Christian. Christianity has countless denomination—41,000 is what I read. The reason why there are 41,000 Christian denominations is not because the Holy Spirit confused everyone. Rather, the devil is the author of confusion, a liar—and seeks to divide, isolate, and conquer God's children. Religion divides people and never saved anyone. Religion kills people spiritually *and* almost literally, as most people find religion boring anyways. A relationship with Jesus Christ alone will save you in this life and for eternity to come. A relationship will bring you life—and life more abundantly!

Jesus is coming back for one church body, not a fragmented body—one body united in love from all four corners of the earth. Jesus is coming back for a church body that is led by the Holy Spirit; "There is one body and one Spirit—just as you were called to the one hope that belongs to your call—one Lord, one faith, one baptism, one God and Father of all, who is over all and through all and in all" (Ephesians 4:4–5).

So what denomination is the right denomination? It says in 1 John 4:2–3, "This is how you can recognize the Spirit of God: Every spirit that acknowledges that Jesus Christ has come in the flesh is from God, but every spirit that does not acknowledge Jesus is not from God." Furthermore, John 3:35–36 says, "The Father loves the Son and has placed everything in his hands. Whoever believes in the Son has eternal life, but whoever rejects the Son will not see life, for God's wrath remains on them."

My Friend Rae

I lost one of my friends to lung and lymph node cancer on July 5, 2019. Raoufa Bazzy was only thirty-nine years old. She suffered for two and a half months before passing from this life. Our lives connected on June 4, 2007, as we were new hires at a large pharmaceutical company. We were hired as drug reps, rookies to the industry. The next two months or so of training were intense, and we became quick friends, as did many in our training class. Trials have a way of bringing people together, and we supported each other and studied together in efforts to make it out of training and into physician offices.

I sometimes mentioned to others that Rae and I went through blood, sweat, and tears together in this job process—and this made Rae laugh and smile. We both were hard workers and determined to make our mark, or at a minimum, not get fired.

Rae was an Arab Muslim, and as I mentioned, I was raised as a Romanian Pentecostal. I noticed many similarities between our cultures. Both were loving, hospitable, loud, friendly, enjoyed great food, and always treated you like family. Not only was my friend Rae this way, but the doctors and staff at the offices we called on in Dearborn, Michigan behaved the same.

Growing up, for Rae and I, how you looked in front of people was very important, perhaps trumping the reality of the situation, and boys got away with more bad things than girls did. We both noticed hypocrisies in the religions and cultures we were brought up in. This is probably the reason why Rae was always open to hearing about my faith in Jesus, talking about the Bible, and also discussing prophecy. She was genuinely interested in faith and prophecy, and in the last text message we communicated, she said, "I'm so sorry. Everything happens for a reason. It's God's plan in the end." This was Rae's response after I told her I had a miscarriage on my 40th birthday.

As I'm writing this, I still can't believe she has passed. I truly miss her. She was one of those people you could easily connect with because she was transparent, fun, loving, and caring. She treated everyone the same—rich doctors and stinky doctors. She made no difference between medical staff and the physicians themselves, treating all with respect and kindness.

I learned about Rae's passing from a colleague, just the day before her funeral and burial. I made it to the cemetery as they lowered my friend into the ground. I asked another gal who Rae's mother was. Rae often talked about her mom; however, I never met her before. I was pointed to a black SUV. Rae's mother had MS and was so weak—especially with the grief from losing her daughter, she couldn't even get out of the vehicle. I walked up, grabbed her hand, and said, "Hi, I'm Tabitha...Rae and I worked together... Rae wanted to bring you to see my house." She nodded yes, as she remembered this. Then I suddenly began to sob terribly. "Rae had a good heart!" I told her mom through the sobs. I touched her shoulder and said, "God bless you," and left the vehicle. Others had lined up behind me to pay respects to her as well.

I am thankful and grateful to God to have known Rae—as a colleague and as a friend. Through this friendship and job, my heart has opened to the Muslim community. My heart's desire is to impact the entire Arab culture for the glory of God! Lord, your will be done in the Arab community, in Jesus' name, amen.

Here in Michigan and especially in Dearborn, there exists the largest population of Arab Muslims in the USA. Certainly there are Muslims around the world too. I did some research on Islam, for it is important to understand where one is coming from, in order to lead them to Christ. The following paragraphs regarding Islam come from gotquestions.org.

The History of Islam

In the seventh century, Muhammad claimed the angel Gabriel visited him. During these angelic visitations, which continued for about twenty-three years until Muhammad's death, the angel purportedly revealed to Muhammad the words of Allah (the Arabic word for God used by Muslims). These dictated revelations compose the Qur'an, Islam's holy book. Islam means "submission," deriving from a root word that means "peace." The word Muslim means "one who submits to Allah."

The Doctrine of Islam

Muslims summarize their doctrine in six articles of faith:

1. Belief in one Allah: Muslims believe Allah is one, eternal, creator, and sovereign.
2. Belief in the angels.
3. Belief in the prophets: the prophets include the biblical prophets but end with Muhammad as Allah's final prophet.
4. Belief in the revelations of Allah: Muslims accept certain portions of the Bible, such as the Torah and the Gospels.

They believe the Qur'an is the preexistent, perfect word of Allah.

5. Belief in the last day of judgment and the hereafter: everyone will be resurrected for judgment into either paradise or hell.

6. Belief in predestination: Muslims believe Allah has decreed everything that will happen. Muslims testify to Allah's sovereignty with their frequent phrase, inshallah, meaning "if God wills."

The Five Pillars of Islam

These five tenets compose the framework of obedience for Muslims:

1. The testimony of faith (shahada): "La ilaha illa allah. Muhammad rasul Allah." This means "There is no deity but Allah. Muhammad is the messenger of Allah." A person can convert to Islam by stating this creed. The shahada shows that a Muslim believes in Allah alone as deity and believes that Muhammad reveals Allah.

2. Prayer (salat): five ritual prayers must be performed every day.

3. Giving (zakat): this almsgiving is a certain percentage given once a year.

4. Fasting (sawm): Muslims fast during Ramadan in the ninth month of the Islamic calendar. They must not eat or drink from dawn until sunset.

5. Pilgrimage (hajj): if physically and financially possible, a Muslim must make the pilgrimage to Mecca in Saudi Arabia at least once. The hajj is performed in the twelfth month of the Islamic calendar.

A Muslim's entrance into paradise hinges on obedience to these Five Pillars. Still, Allah may reject them. Even Muhammad was not sure whether Allah would admit him to paradise (Surah 46:9).

An Evaluation of Islam

Compared to Christianity, Islam has some similarities but significant differences. Like Christianity, Islam is monotheistic. However, Muslims reject the Trinity—that God has revealed Himself as one in three Persons: the Father, Son, and Holy Spirit.

Muslims claim that Jesus was one of the most important prophets—not God's Son. Islam asserts that Jesus, though born of a virgin, was created like Adam. Muslims do not believe Jesus died on the cross. They do not understand why Allah would allow His prophet Isa (the Islamic word for Jesus) to die a torturous death. Yet the Bible shows how the death of the perfect Son of God was essential to pay for the sins of the world (Isaiah 53:5–6; John 3:16, 14:6; 1 Peter 2:24).

Islam teaches that the Qur'an is the final authority and the last revelation of Allah. The Bible, however, was completed in the first century with the book of Revelation. The Bible warns against anyone adding to or subtracting from God's Word (Deuteronomy 4:2; Proverbs 30:6; Galatians 1:6–3931 12; Revelation 22:18). The Qur'an, as a claimed addition to God's Word, directly disobeys God's command.

Muslims believe that paradise can be earned through keeping the Five Pillars. The Bible, in contrast, reveals that sinful man can never measure up to the holy God (Romans 3:23, 6:23). Only by God's grace may sinners be saved through repentant faith in Jesus (Acts 20:21, Ephesians 2:8–9).

Because of these essential differences and contradictions, Islam and Christianity cannot both be true. The Bible and Qur'an cannot both be God's Word. The truth has eternal consequences.

"Beloved, do not believe every spirit, but test the spirits to see whether they are from God, because many false prophets have gone out into the world. By this you know the Spirit of God: every spirit that confesses that Jesus Christ has come in the flesh is from God; and every spirit that does not confess Jesus is not from God; this is the spirit of the antichrist, of which you have heard that it is coming, and now it is already in the world" (1 John 4:1–4; see also John 3:35–36; Gotquestions.org).

Let's pray, believe, and look for opportunities to impact our Arab friends. God can use us if we make ourselves available to His service. It is quite simple. You may be at a park with your family; you can ask God then and there to give you an opportunity to share. You can pray each morning, "Lord, use me today to be your hands and feet, in Jesus' name." We tend to think sharing Jesus is complicated—it isn't. Just like you can easily talk to someone about your favorite sports team, you can naturally share Christ. Make it a normal part of your conversation. God's will and God's heart is for *all* to come to the revelation that Jesus is Lord and Savior! Let's have God's heart—an open loving heart—to reach all people for God's glory!

Chapter 3

The Holy Spirit

God the Father, Jesus His Son, and the Holy Spirit are separate but work in complete harmony—as if all three are actually one. All three were together from the beginning, as we learned in chapter one.

Because the Father, the Son, and the Holy Spirit are one, I believe when you get saved, you receive all three. However, there is more to the story. There is the *baptism* or filling of the Holy Spirit, which we will discuss in this chapter.

But first, let's look at what Jesus said regarding the Holy Spirit. During the time Jesus was on earth, when His time to be crucified drew near, he spoke about the Holy Spirit to his disciples:

> If you love me, keep my commands. And I will ask the Father, and he will give you another advocate to help you and be with you forever—the Spirit of truth. The world cannot

accept him, because it neither sees him nor knows him. But you know him, for he lives with you and will be in you. I will not leave you as orphans; I will come to you. (John 14:15–18)

But the Helper, the Holy Spirit, whom the Father will send in my name, he will teach you all things and bring to your remembrance all that I have said to you. Peace I leave with you; my peace I give to you. Not as the world gives do I give to you. Let not your hearts be troubled, neither let them be afraid. (John 14:26–27)

But when the Helper comes, whom I will send to you from the Father, that is the Spirit of Truth who comes from the Father, He will testify and bear witness about Me. But you will testify also and be My witnesses, because you have been with Me from the beginning. (John 15:26–27)

But now I am going to him who sent me, and none of you asks me, "Where are you going?" But because I have said these things to you, sorrow has filled your heart. Nevertheless,

I tell you the truth: it is to your advantage that I go away, for if I do not go away, the Helper will not come to you. But if I go, I will send him to you. And when he comes, he will convict the world concerning sin and righteousness and judgment: concerning sin, because they do not believe in me; concerning righteousness, because I go to the Father, and you will see me no longer; concerning judgment, because the ruler of this world is judged. I still have many things to say to you, but you cannot bear them now. When the Spirit of truth comes, he will guide you into all the truth, for he will not speak on his own authority, but whatever he hears he will speak, and he will declare to you the things that are to come. He will glorify me, for he will take what is mine and declare it to you. All that the Father has is mine; therefore I said that he will take what is mine and declare it to you. (John 16:5–15)

Even before Jesus spoke these rich words regarding the Holy Spirit, He lays some groundwork. First, Jesus introduces His disciples to a *new commandment;* "A new commandment I give to you, that you love one another; as I have loved you, that you also love one another. By this all will know that you are My disciples, if you have love for one another" (John 13: 34–35). Remember, the end of Christ's life draws near and He is imparting to His own some last words—some *very important* last words, that we must grab a hold of also. *Love is the foundation and the essence of Christianity.* Love for your brother, love for all people, is possible. But you have to long for it. You must desire this perfect love to exist in your being. Jesus taught us how to love, and as we read about His example in the Word, we can do likewise.

Next, Jesus reassures His disciples that although He will be leaving soon, He will also return; "Let not your heart be troubled; you believe in God, believe also in Me. In My Father's house are many mansions, if it were not so, I would have told you. I go to prepare a place for you. And if I go and prepare a place for you, I will come again and receive you to Myself; that where I am, there you may be also. And where I go you know, and the way you know" (John 14: 1–4).

Then, the last teaching Jesus gave His disciples before teaching on the Holy Spirit was about *works*. Our works, our actions, what we spend our time doing…matters. Scripture says, If someone believes in Jesus, they will do the same works as Jesus, and even greater works. And anything one asks in Jesus' name, He will do it (John 14:12–14).

Afterward, Jesus begins to talk about the Holy Spirit, as we read in the passages above.

So who is the Holy Spirit? First, the Holy Spirit is the *Spirit of truth*, who will teach us all things, guide us into all truth, and remain with us forever. If there has ever been a need for truth, *today* truth is needed like never before. Jesus says in John 8:31–32, "If you abide in my word, you are truly my disciples, and you will know the truth, and the truth will set you free." Jesus was the Word of Truth that became flesh, and the Holy Spirit testifies and bears witness of this, and brings to remembrance all Jesus says in His Word. Love, obedience, and truth seem to go hand-in-hand throughout scripture.

Jesus also refers to the Holy Spirit as *the Helper* and comforter. I'm reminded of the first couple, when God saw that it was not good for Adam to be alone, and He created Eve, a helper for him. Contrary to popular belief, the word *helper* is not a demeaning word, but a powerful word. Before Eve, Adam was incomplete. Had he been complete, there wouldn't have been any reason for God to create Eve. Eve's role as a helper was essential and critical. Adam was the head (there can only be one head); and Eve was the helper, in many ways like a compass. Likewise, the Helper, the Holy Spirit, is an internal compass, helping us walk in the ways of the Lord. Without Him, we are playing the guessing game, stumbling along aimlessly.

69

Next, the Holy Spirit is our *advocate*, like a lawyer in many respects. Advocate defined is one who pleads the cause of another, one who defends or maintains a cause or proposal (www.merriam-webster.com). Paul writes in Romans 8:26–27, "In the same way, the Spirit helps us in our weakness. We do not know what we ought to pray for, but the Spirit himself intercedes for us through wordless groans. And he who searches our hearts knows the mind of the Spirit, because the Spirit intercedes for God's people in accordance with the will of God." What does it mean to intercede? It means to intervene between parties with a view to reconcile differences: mediate (www.merriam-webster.com).

The Holy Spirit is also referred to as the *anointing oil* (Exodus 30 and Matthew 25). When something is lubricated, the friction is eliminated (when two objects are in contact with each other), the squeaks go away, and flexibility remains intact—like in the case of a car's motor, a door hinge, and moisturized leather or renewed wineskin. "Once a wineskin has been emptied of all the old wine, it becomes dry, hard and brittle. The wineskin needs to be submerged in water for a period of time. Then, it has oil poured onto it and the oil is massaged into the leather to renew it and make it pliable again" (www.restoringthewell.org). Likewise, the oil or the Holy Spirit in a Christian's life allows a person to be pliable and flexible, not rigid, but full of joy—properly representing the kingdom of God to others. The oil eradicates bitterness and strife, bringing newness of life. Who said that fun is for the world and Christianity is boring? Not so. God is life in abundance and God is fun; and by His powerful Holy Spirit, He resides in us, God's own children.

The Holy Spirit tells us the times we are living in now, and things to come in the future, as we see in the book of Revelation. Furthermore, in Mark 13, Jesus talks about the end times and persecution of God's people, and how or in what manner to defend ourselves; "Whenever you are arrested and brought to trial, do not worry beforehand about what to say. Just say whatever is given you at the time, for it is not you speaking, but the Holy Spirit."

Lastly, the Holy Spirit convicts the world of sin, upholds righteousness, and executes just judgments. How does the Holy Spirit do this? The Holy Spirit resides in God's own children, and uses His children as vessels for His glory and His purposes.

When I think about Jesus telling His disciples, "I must leave so the Holy Spirit can come," it makes me wonder why the Holy Spirit wasn't given *before* Jesus went to be with the Father, while He was still on earth. I believe the answer lies in the parable of motherhood. I find that when I'm with my children (tending to them, teaching them, and loving on them), I am their center, and they are pretty dependent on me. Their dad

71

can be home, however, they always find me. Occasionally when I grocery shop alone, they have no choice but to man up and be more independent, because whomever is watching them is not going to give them the type of attention that (usually) only a mom can and will ever provide. If you are a mama, you are nodding your head yes. If you are a dad, you are probably also nodding your head yes.

But this is not necessarily a bad thing. As a mom, *I must go* at times, so that my kids can let go of me and grow, develop, and mature. How devastating would it be if our kids never matured to the level where they could confidently face life's challenges?

In a similar way, I believe *Jesus had to go.* The disciples and the crowds were clinging to Him. Wherever Jesus went, the disciples and people followed. Can you blame them? Wherever Jesus was, the needs of the people were met—the sick were healed, all sins were forgiven, physical bodies were fed with miraculous food, and the people felt their hearts were warm when in the presence of Jesus. There was peace in the presence of Jesus. Had Jesus stayed on earth for another thirty-three years, you can imagine how many millions of people would be following Jesus around, longing to be in His presence. His disciples and new believers were satisfied with Jesus, and were not looking for anything else.

Once Jesus was taken away, the believers now had a void, a longing for the presence of Jesus. Jesus went *up* and now the Father could send *down* the Holy Spirit. Now Jesus, by the Holy Spirit, could multiply himself in as many people as believed. A Christian in Greece, and a Christian in America, could be in the presence of God; taught by God, led by God, loved by God, and comforted by the Lord—simultaneously. What a wonder this is!

Before the Holy Spirit was given, the embodiment of the Holy Spirit was seen at Jesus' water baptism; "Now when all the people were baptized, and when Jesus also had been baptized and was praying, the heavens were opened, and the Holy Spirit descended on him in bodily form, like a dove; and a voice came from heaven, "You are my beloved Son; with you I am well pleased" (Luke 3). Even before this magnificent event, Elizabeth, John the Baptist's mother, was filled with the Holy Spirit when she heard the voice of Mary, her Lord's mother; and John leaped in her womb and mom and baby were *filled* with the Holy Spirit (Luke 1:41, 15).

The Holy Spirit was *first given to the Jews* on the day of Pentecost. Before this major event happened, the Holy Spirit was promised to come, by Jesus Himself, as He spoke to them shortly before being taken up to heaven before their eyes; "Do not leave Jerusalem, but wait for the gift my Father promised, which you have heard me speak about. For John baptized with water, but in a few days you will be baptized with the Holy Spirit" (Acts 1). After ten days, the Holy Spirit came down from heaven in a powerful way; "When the day of Pentecost came, they were all together in one place. Suddenly a sound like a mighty rushing wind came and filled the entire house where they were sitting. They saw what seemed to be tongues of fire that separated and came to rest on each of them. All of them were *filled* with the Holy Spirit and began to speak in other tongues as the Spirit enabled them" (Acts 2). "About one hundred and twenty followers of Christ (Acts 1:15) were present, including the Twelve Apostles (Matthias was Judas' replacement) (Acts 1:13, 26), Jesus' mother Mary, other female disciples and his brothers (Acts 1:14)" (wikipedia.org).

Later, in Acts 11, the Holy Spirit was also *given to the gentiles*. Peter writes of this; "As I began to speak, the Holy Spirit came on them as he had come on us at the beginning. Then I remembered what the Lord had said: 'John baptized with water, but you will be baptized with the Holy Spirit.' So if God gave them the same gift he gave us who believed in the Lord Jesus Christ, who was I to think that I could stand in God's way? When they heard this, they had no further objections and praised God, saying, "So then, even to Gentiles God has granted repentance that leads to life."

I'd like to focus on some key words from this amazing event *(the promise of the Holy Spirit being fulfilled)*: the gift my Father promised, baptized with the Holy Spirit, filled with the Holy Spirit, and water baptism. Baptism with the Holy Spirit and filled with the Holy Spirit seem to be synonymous, while water baptism is a separate event. The Holy Spirit was *with* the early church before Pentecost, however, after Pentecost the Holy Spirit was available to be received, as a gift is received, inside of one's self; ".....For he lives with you and will be in you" (John 14).

The baptism of the Holy Spirit was also accompanied with the evidence of speaking in tongues—on the day of Pentecost and later when the Holy Spirit came on the gentiles. Acts 2 explains that, "God has raised this Jesus to life, and we are all witnesses of it. Exalted to the right hand of God, he has received from the Father the promised Holy Spirit and has poured out what you now see and hear." The Holy Spirit is described as being *poured out*, hence being *filled* with the Spirit, and that this act was something you could *see* and *hear*, or there was a certain way to recognize this event as having taken place.

Separately from the day of Pentecost, Saul's conversion happens in Acts 9 and we see that Saul believed, then days later received the filling of the Holy Spirit, and was separately baptized in water—three separate events; "So Ananias departed and entered the house. And laying his hands on him he said, "Brother Saul, the Lord Jesus who appeared to you on the road by which you came has sent me so that you may regain your sight and *be filled* with the Holy Spirit." And immediately something like scales fell from his eyes...and he regained his sight. Then he rose and was baptized; and taking food, he was strengthened." In this case, we do not see any evidence of Saul speaking in tongues (although he later writes in 1 Corinthians 14:18 that he speaks in tongues more than them all). However, we do see *evidence*—something like scales that fell from his eyes. And Saul started to preach about Jesus immediately afterward in the synagogues, a sign of receiving the Holy Spirit; "But you will receive power when the Holy Spirit comes on you; and you will be my witnesses in Jerusalem, and in all Judea and Samaria, and to the ends of the earth" (Acts 1:8).

The Holy Spirit is power! Power for what? Power to make disciples. Luke 24:49 says, "And behold, I am sending the promise of my Father upon you. But stay in the city until you are clothed with power from on high." You can't mistake receiving the filling of the Holy Spirit. It is power, not of human nature, but power from on high. The power will *equip* you to share Jesus with others and it will *compel* you to share that the only salvation available to mankind is Jesus Christ.

One must desire, ask, believe, and receive—the gift, the filling, the baptism of the Holy Spirit. Matthew 7:11 says, "If you, then, though you are evil, know how to give good gifts to your children, how much more will your Father in heaven give good gifts to those who *ask* him!" In Acts 19, when Paul came to Ephesus, he found some disciples and asked them, "Did you receive the Holy Spirit when you believed?" And they said, "No, we have not even heard that there is a Holy Spirit." After they were baptized in the name of Jesus, Paul laid his hands on the believers and they were filled with the Holy Spirit—speaking in tongues and prophesying. Furthermore, in Acts 8:17, we learn about the laying on of hands preceding the receival of the Holy Spirit; "Then Peter and John placed their hands on them, and they received the Holy Spirit."

I was baptized in water, and three months later received the baptism of the Holy Spirit, when an elder laid his hand on my head. I was longing and praying for the baptism of the Holy Spirit for about two months, and fervently praying with others seeking the same, at evening prayer meetings. On my own, I just could not receive the gift. I would leave disappointed and didn't know why God would not baptize me. Then at a Tuesday evening prayer meeting, the Holy Spirit led a mature Christian, not an ordained elder but a wonderful mature Christian man, to lay his hand on my head. Instantly, these scriptures from Acts were fulfilled in my life, and I received the filling of the Holy Spirit with the evidence of speaking in tongues. I know others received the baptism of the Holy Spirit when they believed, and spoke in tongues in the confinement of their home, alone. I believe this takes even more faith.

The baptism of the Holy Spirit is for you too, and every believer. After salvation, it is of utmost importance. Our job is to *receive* the Holy Spirit and get to know His voice internally, and come into agreement with what He is saying. There is power in agreement.

After you have been filled with the Spirit, be aware that the devil likes to use fear against God's children. I believe, for this reason, many times *Jesus tells us not to fear.* When teaching about the Holy Spirit, Jesus says in different passages; "Peace I give, Let your hearts not be troubled, Do not fear, Do not be afraid." Opening up to the spiritual opens you up to the possibility of good and evil, and we must guard our hearts and minds with the Word of God, and be vigilant of our thoughts. The devil will attempt to attack you in your thoughts. Any thought that enters your mind that does not line up with scripture, you immediately cast out. We have to learn to detect fear and rebuke it in Jesus' name. Do not be afraid, do not walk in fear. Apply God's Word against the fear and it must flee and will flee.

Once you believe in Jesus, ask to be water baptized, and receive the baptism of the Holy Spirit by the laying on of hands by the church elders. When you walk in the Spirit, you will not fulfill the lust of the flesh (Galatians 5:16).

What are the lusts or works of the flesh? They are: "adultery, fornication, uncleanness, lewdness, idolatry, sorcery, hatred, contentions, jealousies, outbursts of wrath, selfish ambitions, dissensions, heresies, envy, murder, drunkenness, revelries, and the like; of which I tell you beforehand, just as I also told you in time past, that those who practice such things will not inherit the kingdom of God" (Galatians 5: 19–21).

On the contrary, God commands us to live by the Spirit, and the works or fruit of the Spirit is love, joy, peace, longsuffering, kindness, goodness, faithfulness, gentleness, and self-control (Galatians 5:22–23).

It is important what we do in and with our bodies, for they are the temple of the Holy Spirit. You and I must present our bodies as a living sacrifice, holy and pleasing to God (Rom. 12:1).

If you are struggling with any sin, ask God for forgiveness; then ask God to fill you with His Holy Spirit, and there will be no room left for the devil to tempt you, because your temple will be filled with the Spirit of God. Notice when you eat enough healthy food (protein, vegetables, fruit and healthy fats), you are less likely to be enticed by a pan of brownies or a bag of chips. Why? Because your appetite was satisfied with something wholesome, and there is little or no room for junk food.

Being baptized with the Holy Spirit does not mean you have arrived; rather you have fulfilled scripture—and now have power and better tools (as well as more responsibilities and rewards) for God's kingdom. In some ways, it is like having an internal FBI agent, but better. The Holy Spirit also has gifts. Let's explore the gifts of the Holy Spirit now.

Gifts of the Holy Spirit

Paul introduces the gifts of the Holy Spirit in Romans 12; "We have different gifts, according to the grace given to each of us. If your gift is prophesying, then prophesy in accordance with your faith; if it is serving, then serve; if it is teaching, then teach; if it is to encourage, then give encouragement; if it is giving, then give generously; if it is to lead, do it diligently; if it is to show mercy, do it cheerfully."

Paul also teaches on spiritual gifts in 1 Corinthians 12, and says, "Now concerning spiritual gifts, brothers, I do not want you to be uninformed. You know that when you were pagans you were led astray to mute idols, however you were led. Therefore I want you to understand that no one speaking in the Spirit of God ever says "Jesus is accursed!" and no one can say "Jesus is Lord" except in the Holy Spirit. Now there are varieties of gifts, but the same Spirit; and there are varieties of service, but the same Lord; and there are varieties of activities, but it is the same God who empowers them all in everyone. To each is given the manifestation of the Spirit for the common good. For to one is given through the Spirit the utterance of wisdom, and to another the utterance of knowledge according to the same Spirit, to another faith by the same Spirit, to another gifts of healing by the one Spirit, to another the working of miracles, to another prophecy, to another the ability to distinguish between spirits, to another various kinds of tongues, to another the interpretation of tongues. All these are empowered by one and the same Spirit, who apportions to each one."

Furthermore, Paul speaks in Ephesians about Christ *ascending* and thereafter giving gifts to men; specifically some apostles, some prophets, some evangelists, and some pastors and teachers (Ephesians 4:7–11). These specific gifts (apostle, prophet, evangelist, pastor, teacher) are important for "the equipping of the saints for the work of ministry, for the edifying of the body of Christ, till we all come to the unity of the faith and of the knowledge of the Son of God, to a perfect man, to the measure of the stature of the fullness of Christ; that we should no longer be children, tossed to and fro and carried about with every wind of doctrine, by the trickery of men, in the cunning craftiness of deceitful plotting, but, speaking the truth in love..." (Eph. 4:12–15). *Let's take a look at each role.*

"Miracles, healings, discerning of spirits, and words of wisdom accompany the office of the **apostle**. They may even prophesy to exhort, comfort, or edify.Apostles clarify foundational doctrines and function as administrators" (writingforjesus.com). Furthermore, "While a disciple is a student, one who learns from a teacher, an apostle is sent to deliver those teaching to others. Apostle means *messenger*, he who is sent" (www.diffen.com).

The apostles of the New Testament are: Thomas, Peter, Matthew, Philip, Andrew, Bartholomew, John, James the Great, Judas Iscariot, Simon, Matthias, James son of Alphaeus, Barnabas, Paul, James the Less, Mark, and Cephas. I recently read Romans 16 again, and found a woman apostle in the New Testament—Junia—along with her husband, Andronicus. *And apostles of today?* Lord, bless your apostles and bring forth more apostles, for your kingdom, for your glory!

Next, a **prophet** is a person who speaks for God, like Moses did. His older sister, Miriam, was a prophet also (Exodus 15:20). He or she is a mouthpiece God uses and nothing is added or subtracted from the Word of the Lord. Research shows major and minor prophets of the Old Testament; these labels are based on the length of the writings by or about the prophet in the Bible, and are not based on the importance of the prophet, for these prophets are all of great importance. *The major prophets are*: Jeremiah, Isaiah, Ezekiel, Daniel, Joshua, Abraham, and Moses. *The minor prophets are*: Hosea, Joel, Amos, Obadiah, Jonah, Micah, Nahum, Habakkuk, Zephaniah, Haggai, Zechariah, and Malachi (britannica.com). "They were ordinary men called by God to prophesy, and that should encourage us"(theunexpectedbtm.wordpress.com).

In the New Testament, some called Jesus a prophet, and certainly He spoke only what God told Him to speak; but He was so much more than a prophet—Jesus was and is the Son of God! Jesus calls John the Baptist a prophet, and more than a prophet, for he was a messenger sent by God to prepare the way for the Lord (Matthew 11:9–11). Acts 13:1 also mentions prophets and teachers, as does Acts 15:32, with Judas and Silas.

What does an **evangelist** do? "An evangelist is someone who carries the gospel of Jesus Christ to cities and places where the gospel is previously unknown" (www.legit.org). When I think of evangelist, I think of Billy Graham. Certainly, our first examples of evangelists are Matthew, Mark, Luke, and John—who wrote the four gospels in the Bible. Lord raise up more people as such to spread the Good News!

Pastors are called by God to care for the flock, like a shepherd (wikipedia.org). "The broader functions of a shepherd was to lead the sheep to pastures and water (Ps 23:1) to protect them from wild animals (1 Sm 17:34–35); and to guard them at night, whether in the open (Lk 2:8) or in sheepfolds (Zph 2:6) where they counted them as they entered the fold (Jr 33:13)"(www.scielo.org). Likewise, a pastor is called by God to teach the Word, to protect, to forewarn, and to *leave the 99* and go after the lost-sheep. What is a lost-sheep? "A lost-sheep is a disadvantaged or marginalized person who can be brought back into the fold with a little effort" (yourdictionary. com).The love shown by a pastor will win the lost-sheep, back.

Lastly, **teachers** help others acquire knowledge, specifically knowledge from the word of God. Teachers bring 2 Timothy 3:16 to life; "All Scripture is breathed out by God and profitable for teaching, for reproof, for correction, and for training in righteousness."

Once you have been filled with the Holy Spirit, the Holy Spirit has spiritual gifts to give to *each one,* and it is important to know what your gift or gifts are. Gifts are given based on God's will. The Holy Spirit distributes spiritual gifts to all as He sees fit. The purpose of spiritual gifts is to edify, not destroy—working all things for the good of the individual and for the good of the body of Christ.

We should desire spiritual gifts that edify the body (1 Corinthians 14:12), like prophecy. The gift of speaking in tongues has been overemphasized, when gifts that edify the body (like prophecy), should be the more desired gifts, for they edify all. Speaking in tongues edifies self, which is essential to strengthen you personally and spiritually; and it edifies others only if there is an interpreter. However, prophesying edifies all who hear, because it is spoken in the language they understand. "Therefore, brethren, desire earnestly to prophesy, and do not forbid to speak with tongues. Let all things be done decently and in order," said Apostle Paul (1 Corinthians 14: 39–40).

As we study the scriptures pertaining to prophesying, one does so by faith; "If your gift is prophesying, then prophesy in accordance with your faith..." (Romans 12). One prophesies in part, and in doing so, is speaking by faith. Paul says in 1 Corinthians 13:9, "For we know in part and we prophesy in part. But when that which is perfect has come, then that which is in part will be done away."

In the Old Testament, the men audibly heard the voice of God, like in the case of Moses and the burning bush or Samuel hearing the voice of God while he was sleeping, and finally responding, "Speak, Lord, for your servant is listening."

In the New Testament, prophecy was performed by faith, by an internal voice. Paul writes in Corinthians, after explaining the use of spiritual gifts in proper order so there isn't any confusion in the church; "If anyone *thinks himself to be a prophet* or spiritual, let him acknowledge that the things which I write to you are the commandments of the Lord" (1 Corinthians 14:37). With time, you will learn the voice of the Holy Spirit and speak what He tells you to speak. This is a step of faith and is done by faith. And we know, "Faith is the substance of things hoped for, the evidence of things unseen." Confirmation that God spoke through you—or did not speak through you—will come later; however, when you speak what God places on your heart, it may sometimes feel like you are stepping off of a cliff. And if you miss the mark—reflect, correct, and ask the Lord for guidance.

I wouldn't focus on titles, rather focus on doing the will of God and hearing His voice internally. Be available for the Holy Spirit to use you at all times. Remember, the Word says to desire to prophesy, for the edification of others. Years ago, when I read this in the scriptures, I prayed for God to use me in this capacity. I prayed ever so softly and with so much fear and trembling; as I was taught that this is a high calling and that the Lord is holy, and we also must be holy.

What is your spiritual gift? A good indicator of what your spiritual gift or gifts are is to ask yourself the question, "What am I passionate about?" My passion or heart's desire since I was a small child was to help people. I enjoyed when others were defended, helped, or better off as a result of my intervention. Search your heart, analyze yourself before God, and He will reveal to you what your spiritual gifts are. Then you can start using them for the glory of God.

There is a high probability that those things you are passionate about *are* the areas God will use you for in His kingdom. Philippians 2:13 says, "For God is working in you, giving you the desire and the power to do what pleases him." Furthermore in Ephesians, we discover; "For we are God's masterpiece. He has created us anew in Christ Jesus, so we can do the good things he planned for us long ago" (Ephesians 2:10). For example, if you are passionate about seeing miracles happen, like the sick being healed or people bound in wheelchairs suddenly rising and receiving healing—this *desire* was probably put there by God, and it is very likely that He planned for you to be used in this way (to miraculously heal the sick in Jesus' name) *long ago.*

If this is your passion, or something different, do your part. First, make sure your motives are pure. God gets all the glory; you are simply an instrument God uses. The joy and fulfillment you will experience, as a result of being an instrument God can use, will be more than enough of a reward from the Lord. All the credit belongs to Him, because it is His power that is at work, not your own power. Secondly, abide in God and His entire word every day; casting out of your heart anger, hatred, bitterness, envy, jealousy, greed, and fear—in Jesus' name. When you sin, repent immediately, and God is always ready to forgive.

Ask God today to reveal to you what your *gift and calling* is! God is faithful and will make it known to you. We have a responsibility as children of God to be filled with the Holy Spirit *and* to use the spiritual gifts He gives us, as part of our daily Christian lives. Paul says in 1 Timothy 4:14, "Do not neglect your gift, which was given you through prophecy when the body of elders laid their hands on you."

Spiritual gifts are needed and necessary, working toward our perfection, edifying the entire body of Christ. The Holy Spirit through us, *those filled with the Spirit*, convicts the world of sin, brings the sin to light, and through love breaks the chains of sin in the life of the sinner—who is desperate for relief. You cannot afford to be lax in this area!

God's Holy Spirit and the gifts of the Holy Spirit operate *accurately* when God's laws are respected and followed in the life of the believer. *Inaccuracy* in prophecy or other spiritual gifts happens when we are not walking in the Spirit, having the fruit of the Spirit. Galatians 5:22–23 says, "But the fruit of the Spirit is love, joy, peace, forbearance, kindness, goodness, faithfulness, gentleness and self-control. Against such things there is no law."

It is not by chance that *love* is the first fruit of the Spirit, and the second is *joy,* then *peace.* In my personal life, once I understood and obeyed the greatest commandments (love God, love your neighbor), I was able to experience true joy, and peace quickly followed. After we are baptized with the Holy Spirit, we *must* grow in baring (revealing, exposing) the fruit of the Spirit. It, the fruit, is in our possession (so to speak), but it must be searched out, looked for, dug up, and polished (to wax, to shine, to brighten). Life's situations cause us either to dig down *or* to remain on the surface. When we dig deeper with God (read your Bible slower and ask God questions where you are unsure; pray without ceasing, even in your mind; fast on a regular basis; and hang out with Christians who love God and love people)—we will begin to uncover the fruit of the Spirit—whom God himself put inside of us. Praise the Lord!

Paul says in Romans 11:29, "For God's gifts and his call are irrevocable" or "without repentance". This means that you can have a spiritual gift, walk in the spirit, and be a pure vessel that God uses for His glory. However, if you are not careful, and you follow the flesh—you can just as likely be an impure vessel, with an inaccurate or only partially accurate message; for the gift remains. If one falls in this trap, repent, and God will restore your spiritual sight and bring accuracy back to your spiritual gift.

The devil would love nothing more than to steer you off course and cause you to error in some way. For example, if you have the gift of prophecy and *add* or *imply* something from yourself willingly, for personal gain, or adding anything at all that will change the overall meaning of the prophecy—this is evil and taints the work of the Holy Spirit, bringing shame to the name of Jesus and God the Father.

Or if you mention to your Christian brother or sister who is seeking counsel from the Lord that others have given you a love offering, as a financial support for you and your family—this is also evil. The power of God can never be used for personal gain (financial or any other gain). If you are lacking financially, pray to God in secret, and God will provide for all of your needs. We are reassured in Psalm 37:25; "I was young and now I am old, yet I have never seen the righteous forsaken or their

90

children begging bread." Through the Holy Spirit, the Lord can place it on brothers' and sisters' hearts, or even through a stranger, to give you money for your need.

Certainly you can share your financial distress with church leadership that can help you; I don't think this is wrong necessarily. However, exchanging spiritual guidance for money is a sin (read 2 Kings 5). Freely you receive; freely you give (Matthew 10:8).

The spiritual gift that comes from the Lord is perfect, and we must treat it as such. Trust Him in all things. Remain pure. You can see why God allowed the thorn to remain in the flesh of apostle Paul. God used Paul, who wrote a big part of the New Testament, in such a large capacity that in order to keep Paul's flesh from being puffed up or prideful, He allowed the *messenger of Satan*, the thorn in his side, to remain in order to keep him humble. Knowing that we are just an instrument that God uses and that God is the one that performs the miracles by His Holy Spirit—will keep us humble and enable God to use us further. I do believe that if you are faithful and show maturity with the gift God gives you, like in the parable with the talents, God will give you even more spiritual gifts.

Baptism with the Holy Spirit and spiritual gifts are scriptural. Both are necessary for all believers, in order for the Church body to reach its full potential in Christ, and in order to carry out the mission of salvation to the ends of the earth. You will know if you received the baptism of the Holy Spirit if you have the accompaniment of speaking in tongues and if you receive power—a boldness to live for the Lord and to be a witness wherever your feet go.

The journey with the Holy Spirit continues every day. We must acknowledge the Holy Spirit and ask the Lord to fill us with His Holy Spirit daily. He is our best friend—don't ignore Him or grieve Him by sinning. The Bible says, "Be filled with the spirit and you will not fulfill the lust of the flesh."

To remain in truth and not be led astray, read your Bible daily and obey what it says. Remember, the Bible and the Holy Spirit work together, never contradicting each other, and always working all things for the good of God's people and for God's glory!

Chapter 4

The Mission of the Church

Jesus was crucified, died, and rose from the dead after three days; thereby defeating death, hell, and the grave. During the *forty days* after His resurrection, He walked the earth and showed himself to hundreds of people, and said the following *last words* before He returned to the Father: "But you will receive power when the Holy Spirit comes upon you. And you will be my witnesses, telling people about me everywhere—in Jerusalem, throughout Judea, in Samaria, and to the ends of the earth" (Acts 1:8). After Jesus spoke these words, He was taken up into a cloud, while they watched (Acts 1:9).

Jesus leaves similar instructions for believers in Matthew 28:18–20, saying, "All authority in heaven and on earth has been given to me. Therefore go and make disciples of all nations, baptizing them in the name of the Father and of the Son and of the Holy Spirit, and teaching them to obey everything I have commanded you. And surely I am with you always, to the very end of the age."

There is a huge responsibility described here in these two different passages. Are we fulfilling our responsibility and obeying Jesus' last instructions—very crucial instructions?

Every company, organization, or entity has a mission statement. More importantly, Christ's church has a mission and a role on this planet. Only with the filling or baptism of the Holy Spirit can we fulfill our mission, fulfill Jesus' command—to go and make disciples of all nations. Remember, one day we will give an account to God. We all want to hear, "Well done, good and faithful servant!"

Certainly, I can't speak for every Christian church in America or globally. However, based on what I've experienced, today's Church is comfortable with the current state it is in. Many people think things are going well. I see it differently. Some churches are merely existing, not growing or thriving. Perhaps some Christians haven't experienced anything different, so there is nothing to compare reality to. Others are growing in numbers. Are they growing spiritually, too, from milk to meat?

In my home church, the number of church members is constant at best, with little to no growth—unless babies are born, or someone gets married and brings their spouse in, or a family moves in from out of town. Unfortunately, we are not growing and doing what Jesus said, to go out and make disciples—disciples of all nations, or nationalities, not just of your own kind. The early church grew daily in numbers.

Many are called, few are chosen

Why aren't we growing? At least in the community I was raised in, I believe the reason lies (at least in part) in the incorrect interpretation of the phrase, "Many are called, but few are chosen." In essence, the false understanding goes like this; "Only a few will be chosen and saved. My family and I are chosen and probably will be qualifiers of salvation because God favors us. The rest of the world that isn't chosen...well, they are not special like us...we are special...praise God." This mentality is false and I will explain why.

If these are your thoughts, how many people will you be incentivized to witness to and try to bring into the kingdom? One, two, none? Our thoughts shape our actions, therefore we must hold thoughts that are true, and abandon falsehood. The entire Bible works together with one heart and one scope—to glorify God and to win as many people as possible for His kingdom. Anything you hear being taught, run it through this filter, run it through other references in the Bible; study an entire book, even an entire person in the Bible, before you draw conclusions on what the author meant—when he wrote what he wrote. For example, Paul wrote a good part of the New Testament. Read all the books he wrote and study them. Understanding the heart of Paul is important in understanding what Paul wrote, and what he was trying to say.

This phrase *many are called, but few are chosen* concludes two parables that Jesus taught to the Jews *(the parable of the workers in the vineyard* and *the parable of the wedding feast)* in trying to get them to understand what the kingdom of God was like. In the latter, the first to be considered, invited or called, was a select group. I believe this select group is the Jews. They refuse, then the invitation goes out to everyone—those considered in society as being good and those in society considered as being bad. Note that the first group and the last group were both *called* or invited, together making up the group of *many are called*.

The very act of the Jews rejecting Jesus paved a way for salvation to be brought to us, the gentiles. This is the main idea of these parables; salvation is for the Jew and for the gentile. Salvation is for all! However, how will we respond to the call, to the invitation for salvation? *You and I* choose to accept or choose to reject—the invitation that Christ extends to all humanity. Joshua expresses in the Old Testament, I imagine ever so passionately, "Choose this day whom you will serve!"

The next part is the end of the day or evening in the first parable (and the day of the wedding celebration in the second parable). I believe this timeframe represents the end of the age. At the end of both of these parables, among other things, Jesus says that *many are called, but few are chosen.* If you look at both parables, and compare and contrast merely by *many versus few*, who would you say is in the group of *many*? The commoners, the unskilled, the nobodies and somebodies of society; everyone else would certainly qualify, right? Were the *many* refused by God? No. In the first parable, the latecomers (gentiles) received the same reward as those who came first (the Jews), those who worked all day. Jesus pays *the last* first, and they received the same salary as *the first*, which made *the first* furious. Jesus did it this way to show what was in the evil hearts of the religious Jews. In the second parable, most of the people that were invited stayed at the wedding celebration. How many were kicked out? One. More importantly, *why* did the one person get kicked out? He lacked a wedding garment.

The evil in their hearts in the first parable, and *the lack of a wedding garment* in the second parable, is what is keeping Jews, and all people for that matter, out of the kingdom of God. If you see yourself as better than others, you can't humble yourself, which is a requirement to approaching the kingdom of God and receiving Christ. And if you think your good works will earn you eternal life, you are wrong. Even our best works are like filthy rags in the sight of God. We must be clothed with Christ, the only acceptable wedding garment.

The only way to enter heaven is through the narrow gate, Jesus Christ, who is the only door to God and eternal life. Jesus talks to the Israelites of the narrow gate in Luke 13, and says, "Strive to enter through the narrow gate." Strive means to struggle or fight vigorously. Why would Jesus tell the Jews to *strive* to enter? I believe the reason is this: For someone reliant on religion, reliant on what they have done or their good works—it is even more difficult to have faith and be saved, for faith requires one to put their trust and reliance on an unseen God, and the works that *He did*, not on my own works.

A few verses down in Luke 13, Jesus continues to speak to the Jews; "There will be weeping and gnashing of teeth, when you see Abraham and Isaac and Jacob and all the prophets in the kingdom of God, and yourselves thrust out. They will come from the east and the west, from the north and the south, and sit down in the kingdom of God. And indeed there are last who will be first, and there are first who will be last."

Who was thrust out of the kingdom of God, as was the man without proper clothing at the wedding, in the parable of the wedding feast? The religious Jews were thrust out.

Note who is together with Abraham, Isaac, and Jacob in the kingdom of God; "They will come from the east and the west, from

98

the north and the south, and sit down in the kingdom of God." Does this seem like a few people or many people? I see many people. Additionally, John 3:16 talks about God's love being sent to all the world, all the people, many people. *For whomever believes in Jesus will have eternal life.*

God and Jesus did their part—show the greatest love possible and die for our sins—and you and I must do our part: Believe in Jesus and remain in Him until the end. There is no favoritism, no other secret formula for salvation. This is it. Therefore, I believe from scripture that anyone can be saved, not just a special group, not just a chosen group. However, a large task stands before us. We must share Jesus with our neighbor. Only after hearing—can a person believe and be saved.

Of the Jewish population, even though salvation is for all Jews, few find Jesus because they are bound in religion, having works as their foundation, when Christ must be the foundation. Paul was bound in religion. Paul thought he was doing the will of God, even though he was doing the opposite of God's will and persecuting Christians. However, Jesus in His perfect plan *chose* Paul on the road to Damascus, and revealed Himself to him. The story of Paul and others chosen by God are unique and rare, hence *few are chosen.* Jesus says of Paul, "He is my chosen instrument" (Acts 9).

After Paul was chosen, he fasted for three days, received the filling or baptism of the Holy Spirit when Ananias laid hands on him, and was afterward water baptized. Likewise, we must follow these *foundations of the faith*. No wonder Paul was able to endure hardships and be used by God in such a powerful way—Paul was filled with the Spirit of God!

We must pray for the salvation of the Jewish race—that their eyes would be opened, that the spirit of religion be broken, in Jesus' name, amen! One must have a relationship with their Maker. Religion is so dangerous. Religion focuses on self, a one-man-team. A relationship is a partnership; you and Jesus hand-in-hand, journeying together. We don't realize how wonderful and miraculous this is—the Spirit of the living God *can* reside in us. Receive Him as a child would, with humility and faith. Then ask for the baptism of the Holy Spirit.

Getting results

Today, I believe the Holy Spirit is dissatisfied and grieved with our progress and results; "Go and make disciples of all nations," Jesus said. What does *go and make disciples of all nations* entail? Disciple comes from a Latin word that means "learner," and discipline comes from one meaning "instruction, knowledge" (Farlex Trivia Dictionary). Believers, new and veterans, must be taught biblical truths. There must be a transfer of knowledge from the mature, say the pastor, to the believer. "The Hebrew word for pastor in the Bible literally means to tend a flock, pasture it, or graze it" (www.whatchristianswanttoknow.com).

Jesus said to Peter, "Feed my sheep." How do you feed someone spiritually? By teaching them the entire Word of God. Before Jesus gave Peter this command, He ate with His disciples an earthly breakfast (in His resurrected body), and then they talked business. First, Jesus asks Peter three times if he loves Him. The *prerequisite* for serving as a pastor, a worship leader, a youth leader, etc, is love in your heart for God the Father, His Son Jesus, and His Holy Spirit. And what is the test of love? It is this; "If you love me, you will obey my commandments." When leadership obeys all of God's commandments, it models godly living to its' church body—and the sheep will follow.

Apostle Paul says in 1 Corinthians 11:1, "And you should imitate me, just as I imitate Christ." More than what I say, my kids imitate what I do—all the time. That is not always a good thing. I'm a work in progress. Do you know how long it takes to undo poor behavior? Not weeks, but years.

Training your children and congregation up in the ways of the Lord, through words and deeds, produces good fruit in their lives—an investment for this life and the next. The Bible says that teachers (I believe this applies to parents also) will be held at a higher level of accountability. It's not only about you. Others are walking in your footsteps, following your example and teaching. Exemplify how to live for Jesus in your worship, in your teaching, in your public life, in your private life, in your home life, and in your career life.

I have seen preachers and pastors skip worship altogether, and just *take the stage* when he is announced. Quite contrarily, the pastor should be the first to worship, leading by example.

Once a believer is taught the Word of God, including water baptism, and desires to be baptized—Jesus says to baptize them in the name of the Father, the Son, and the Holy Spirit. The desire to be baptized comes from the believer, from the heart—not by force or manipulation of any kind, and not for the sake of showing on paper that annual church baptisms grew by the hundreds or thousands.

A good example of this is the story in the Bible about the eunuch; "As Philip explained the gospel, the Ethiopian eunuch believed. When they came to some water by the side of the road, the eunuch asked to be baptized" (Acts 8:36).

Jesus calls us to be a *growing church*, literally and spiritually—not just filling up church seats (although that is an ambitious and notable start). We need to bring people in, baptize them, and teach them to obey the Word of God (Matthew 28: 18–20).I have found that quite a few American Christian churches have been successful at bringing people in. This is an awesome thing. How do they do it? From what I've noticed, these churches try to connect with people, have talented worship services, and have attention-grabbing sermon titles. On the surface, I see nothing wrong with this, as some critics do—as long as God is the center of everything that happens, and repentance and obedience to the entire Bible are taught to its congregation.

There was a season in my life, for a few months, when I listened to the sermons of a well-known megachurch pastor. And they were helpful to me. There is a purpose for positive sermons. This is why I cannot jump on the bandwagon that says, "Megachurches and megachurch worship teams are of the devil," like some may say or think.

However, after a few months, I had to dig deeper. Looking back, I was being fed milk, but it was what I needed at the time. Feeding someone milk, like a baby, is appropriate. The problem arises when you continue to feed milk to an adult. Pastors have a responsibility to take their members from feeding on milk to feeding on meat. How? By teaching the entire Bible, not just the benefits, not just positive scriptures, but teaching believers to obey everything that God says in

His Word. Teach that blessing follows after obedience. Confession and repentance are critical parts of being a Christian and essential for being set free from sin. Sin is cancer in the human heart and must come out, and hearts must be washed with the Word. The prosperity movement preached blessings, but didn't always teach the prerequisite for blessings—obedience to God's Word. I heard a preacher say once, "God will not bless your mess," or God will not bless your state of disobedience. Obedience will be more attainable once a believer is baptized or filled with God's Holy Spirit. Fast, desire, ask, believe—until you receive the baptism of the Holy Spirit!

Consider this example, as we look at *positive preaching* from a different angle. You are not feeling well and decide to schedule a doctor's visit to ensure nothing serious is going on. The appointment day comes, and they do a variety of tests and scans. The nurse also draws blood and sends it off to the lab. You wait impatiently for the results. Finally, the results come back, and all the tests show you have a cancerous tumor. But the doctor decides that this news will be too hard to deliver, and too difficult for you to handle, so the doctor comes in and says, "Everything looks great!"

In like manner, people from outside of the church, that come inside of the church, are coming for a reason. They've come for a *spiritual check-up*. Something on the inside isn't sitting right and somehow they've made it into a church seat. There is sin, much like a tumor or cancer, in the human heart. This tumor must be removed, or else the person will die. Each person deserves to know the whole truth, so they can take appropriate actions. Telling people only positive things, like God loves you, *which He absolutely does*; but neglecting to also tell people that God is holy, and neglecting to show them how to live for the Creator of the universe in a holy way—is a huge disservice with eternal consequences.

Another *mission of the church* is to heal the sick. Healings of any disease, great or small, should be a normal part of church and the norm in the life of all Christians; "And these signs will accompany those who believe: In My name they will drive out demons; they will speak in new tongues; they will pick up snakes with their hands, and if they drink any deadly poison, it will not harm them; they will lay their hands on the sick, and they will be made well" (Mark 16:16–18). Take notice these are the qualities of all Christians—*all*. We must examine ourselves to ensure we are in the faith, totally on fire for the Lord. The kingdom must be our focus—and everything else falls in second place. Then, He will give us strength, courage, and power to lay hands on the sick and see them recover, in the name of Jesus.

In May of 2020, my father-in-law was discharged covid positive from the hospital, and he came to stay with us. Even though the doctor and nursing staff that treated him showed up to the house in what looked like hazmat suits, we did not as much as wear a mask, as the virus is so small and passes right through—so what's the point. Guess what? All six of us were a-okay. Even before we took him in, I had so much strength knowing that we were doing what God wanted us to do, that God was protecting us, and no harm would fall on any of us. The scripture from Mark 16 came to life: God can and does give us supernatural ability over sickness and disease. However, when we do get sick, when we do contract viruses (I contracted covid about a year later), God is still with us, and we can feel His comfort and presence—even in the midst of suffering.

I lay hands on myself and my kids, for God to grant healing and give us peace. Once, I had a rather large cyst that was seen by doctors on ultrasound and physical exam. What prompted the visit to the doctor was my continuous bleeding for over four weeks. The doctor recommended I schedule another appointment to talk about the next step. The day before my next appointment, I was praying in tongues, worshipping God, and I felt led by the Holy Spirit to place my hands on the core of my body. I prayed God would touch me and heal me. That day, the bleeding stopped and the next day when the doctor attempted to reexamine the cyst, there was no cyst to reexamine. God had touched my body, yesterday, and removed it by the power of His Holy Spirit. Praise to His name forever!

Furthermore, in our first year of marriage, we started a new business. This came with stress as well, and one day my husband felt very overwhelmed and fearful. He asked if I would pray for him and I was glad to do it. I prayed and the power of God took away the fear instantly.Praise to His name forever!

Lastly, I have prayed for people and seemingly nothing happened. However, this doesn't stop me from believing and praying. I lay hands on whomever accepts and desires to be prayed for. I do my part, and that's all God requires from each one of us. We pray, we believe, and then leave the situation in God's hands. This is our mission; this is the calling for all Christians—to lay hands on the sick and see the sick recover.

Even greater works

Wherever Jesus went, people found Him by the thousands. Why did they seek Him out? Because He met their needs—physical and spiritual. Jesus had authority and power. John 14 explains that we, the body of Christ, have the same power to do the same works Christ did, and even greater works; "I tell you the truth, anyone who believes in me will do the same works I have done, and even greater works, because I am going to be with the Father. You can ask for anything in my name, and I will do it, so that the Son can bring glory to the Father. Yes, ask me for anything in my name, and I will do it!" (John 14:12–14).

I spent some time pondering what *greater works will you do* means. But first, Jesus says we will do *the same works*. What works did Jesus do?

❖ Jesus has turned water into wine (John 2:1–11).

❖ He has read the mind of the woman of Samaria (John 4:18).

❖ He has healed the official's son (John 4:46–54).

- ❖ He had healed the man crippled for thirty-eight years (John 5:1–9).

- ❖ He had fed five thousand people with five loaves and two fish (John 5:1–14).

- ❖ He had walked on water (John 6:19).

- ❖ He had healed a man born blind (John 9:1–7).

- ❖ He had raised Lazarus from the dead after four days in the grave (John 11:43–44).

(desiringgod.org)

Everything Jesus did—all of His works, all of His actions, and all of His deeds reflected God the Father and pointed back to the Father. Likewise, all of our works must always reflect God and point to the Father. Man takes no credit. Rather, all credit belongs to God, who is the one performing miracles through us. Praise to His name forever!

So Jesus says, "You will do the same works," and continues to say, "Even greater works will you do because I go to be with the Father." Remember, Jesus went to be with the Father and after ten days, God sent His Holy Spirit (Acts 2).

In essence, I believe Jesus is saying that the reason we will be able to do *even greater works* is based on the Holy Spirit dwelling in believers; "Nevertheless, I tell you the truth. It is to your advantage that I go away; for if I do not go away, the Helper will not come to you; but if I depart, I will send Him to you" (John 16:7). I have heard it preached before that God is a God of multiplication, and based on His word, this is true. In essence, Jesus multiplied Himself, by the Holy Spirit, in the hearts of all who would only believe (and abide in Him).

It is important to note that in order to do the same works, and even greater works than Jesus did, we must have faith and believe. Through our *unbelief,* we actually stop the hand of God from moving; "And because of their unbelief, he couldn't do any miracles among them except to place his hands on a few sick people and heal them" (Mark 6:5). We *must* have faith and believe. And when we don't, we must cry out to God; "Lord, help my unbelief!"

The Holy Spirit dwelling in Christians is what guides us, strengthens us, instructs us, gives us wisdom beyond what humans are capable of, gives us wings for rapture, and allows each of us to do the works that God called us to do—all at the same time, around the globe. That is magnificent!

The purpose of all works, great or small, are to point people to Jesus, and from Jesus to God. When a sick person gets healed or even if a person is raised from the dead, it should always point to God and be for the glory of God. The miracles or works are just to get people's attention and help them believe. God wants your heart. God wants you to belong to Him for eternity.

The Holy Spirit in us performs the same works that Jesus did, and even greater works. False miracles, weird doctrine, and anything that is not found in scripture has given the Church a bad reputation and must be abandoned. For example, I can recall two times in the New Testament, when people fell backward, flat to the floor. First, when they came to arrest Jesus; "When Jesus said to them, "I am he," they drew back and fell to the ground" (John 18:6). Then, in the case of Ananias and Sapphira—and it was because they lied to the Holy Spirit, and literally fell flat to the floor and died. When Jesus or the apostles touched and healed people, there was no one falling over or blacking out. *True* miracles exist and will cause unbelievers to become believers, in Jesus' name!

I believe once the body of Christ is baptized with the Holy Spirit—the Spirit of truth—and united in love, true miracles will happen in Christian churches. People from the outside will come by the thousands, God willing millions—however many He will draw in. John 12:32 says, "And I, if I am lifted up from the earth, will draw all peoples to Myself." Likewise, I believe unbelievers will come to us, once we are living the truth from God's Word. People will not come for the light show or smoke machine or any other flesh-appealing mechanisms that are out there. People will come for the presence of God! Isn't that what we want?

God equips us with His Holy Spirit, with power, to go and make disciples of all nations—including family members, friends, and co-workers. The Holy Spirit compels and equips us to share truth with others. He equips us to drive out demons, casting them into the lake of fire, never to return. The Holy Spirit equips us to lay our hands on the sick and see them recover (Mark 16:17–19). Let us obey Jesus' last instructions—making as many disciples as possible—for the glory of God!

Chapter 5

True Worshipers

If you have ever been to a Christian church service, there probably was a time designated to *praise and worship*. Some churches believe that praise and worship songs, in order to be spiritual, should be conducted and performed in a certain fashion or style. Others believe praise songs are fast, and then they switch to slow songs, which they consider worship songs. But why do we praise God and what is really the essence of worship? What does it mean to be a true worshiper?

Praise and worship is very important in God's house and in our daily lives. The deeper my relationship with the Lord, the more I find myself singing spiritual songs; and even from morning time, a song will be on my heart, and I will begin to sing it. Andrew Wommack puts it like this; "Praise affects you, it affects the devil, and it affects God. It touches everything and every part of your life. Likewise, a lack of Praise affects you in a negative way, turns the devil loose in your life, and doesn't bless God. You have to get this area of your life right."

There are countless scriptures I looked at, dedicated to praise and worship. When the praises of God's people went up, the walls of Jericho came down. To **Praise** is to boast, to rave (about), to commend, to speak well of, to laud (fromtheshores. com). When I think of praising someone, I think of the words, "Way to go!" In regards to the kingdom, when we praise God, we are in essence saying, "Way to go, God!" I have witnessed people at sporting events, shouting at the top of their lungs, cheering on their favorite team. How much more, God deserves to be cheered and praised! Let's take a deeper look at just a handful of scriptures on praise.

1. Praise the Lord! Praise God in his sanctuary; praise him in his mighty heavens! (Psalm 150:1)

2. Praise him for his mighty deeds; praise him according to his excellent greatness! Praise him with trumpet sound; praise him with lute and harp! Praise him with tambourine and dance; praise him with strings and pipe! Praise him with sounding cymbals; praise him with loud clashing cymbals. (Psalm 150: 2-5)

3.   Give thanks to the Lord with the lyre; make melody to him with the harp of ten strings! Sing to him a new song; play skillfully on the strings, with loud shouts. (Psalm 33:2–3)

4.   And David and all Israel were rejoicing before God with all their might, with song and lyres and harps and tambourines and cymbals and trumpets. (1 Chronicles 13:8)

5.   O Lord, you are my God; I will exalt you; I will praise your name, for you have done wonderful things, plans formed of old, faithful and sure. (Isaiah 25:1)

6.   Oh sing to the Lord a new song, for he has done marvelous things! His right hand and His holy arm have worked salvation for him. (Psalm 98:1)

7.   My mouth is filled with your praise, and with your glory all the day. (Psalm 71:8)

8.   Why am I discouraged? Why is my heart so sad? I will put my hope in God! I will praise him again—my Savior and my God! (Psalm 42:11)

While studying several dozen scriptures on praise, I found that praises to God include joyful noises, loud singing and shouting, spontaneous songs of praise that are personal—with clapping, dancing, and various instruments being skillfully played. These scriptures paint a picture of a great and wonderful celebration!

The object of praise is God; He gets all the glory and no one else. In fact, God sits on a throne of praises of the Israelites, and God says it is good to sing songs of praise. We should praise the Lord all the time because He deserves our praise! We must lift a sacrifice of praise—meaning, my flesh doesn't always feel like praising, but I will praise Him anyways.

All creation is to praise God—people, angels, hosts, animals—all the earth, the heavens, and all created things that exist in the universe praise the one true God! Try to start singing in the morning, and praise Him all day long (in your heart and mind); praise Him from your soul. Sing with a thankful and glad heart; make melody in your heart, not just with your lips. Sing a new song, and sing thanks to God. Sing about His wondrous works, His strength, and His steadfast love and justices.

A song of praise is not a song about what is breaking your heart. When praising God, replace mourning with dancing and sackcloth with gladness. I didn't find verses teaching to sing about our troubles. We are to cast our cares upon the Lord in prayer, not sing about them. Faith arises when we sing scripture. There are many powerful Christian songs today, taken right from scripture.

Now, let's do a temperature check. How does our personal praises to God compare to what these bible passages describe? I know I have to step it up in the area of praising God. Furthermore, what does praise look like in your home church? I think it is safe to say, there is room for improvement in every church. We should strive to reach the level King David reached in praising God; "Wearing a linen ephod, David was dancing before the Lord with all his might" (2 Samuel 6:14). Remember, David was a man after God's own heart. I would love to have a glimpse at what David's dancing looked like. *David danced with all his might.* Certainly there was movement—perhaps dancing in circles and clapping. Without a doubt, David's dancing was non-sensual, and not like we see the world doing today at clubs and such. David's dancing, just like his singing, was an expression of what was in his heart; and he was bringing praise to God! Like it or not, it's in there and painted all over the psalms.

I believe when God's people are so full of the Holy Spirit, singing and clapping will not be enough for us to express the joy of the Lord, and to fully express what we are feeling inside of our hearts, we will begin to dance before the Lord!

Now, let's study worship. What does it mean to worship? **Worship** by definition means extravagant respect or admiration for or devotion to an object of esteem. True worship is worshiping the Father in spirit and in truth. Let's take a look at some passages on worship.

1.   But the hour is coming, and is now here, when the true worshipers will worship the Father in spirit and truth, for

the Father is seeking such people to worship him. (John 4:23)

2. I appeal to you therefore, brothers, by the mercies of God, to present your bodies as a living sacrifice, holy and acceptable to God, which is your spiritual worship. (Romans 12:1)

3. Ascribe to the Lord the glory due his name; worship the Lord in the splendor of holiness. (Psalm 29:2)

4. Then Abraham said to his young men, "Stay here with the donkey; I and the boy will go over there and worship and come again to you." (Genesis 22:5)

5. Exalt the Lord our God; worship at his footstool! Holy is he. (Psalm 99:5)

6. The earth is the Lord's and the fullness thereof, the world and those who dwell therein, for he has founded it upon the seas and established it upon the rivers. Who shall ascend the hill of the Lord? And who shall stand in his holy place? He who has clean hands and a pure heart, who does not lift up his soul to what is false and does not swear deceitfully. He will receive blessing from the Lord and righteousness from the God of his salvation. (Psalm 24:1–10)

True worship is all about the Lord, and all about the state of your heart—He's looking into your heart and finding that your heart is completely surrendered and devoted to Him! Worship is a lifestyle, not just a Sunday thing, not just when I'm singing or praying. Worship is obeying the Lord in all things, even if it means giving it all up, as we see with Abraham and his son Isaac. A lifestyle of reading God's Word, and obeying what it says, is a must. "To worship God in spirit and truth necessarily involves loving Him with heart, soul, mind, and strength" (gotquestions. org).

The opposite of *spirit and truth* is *flesh and falsehood*. The flesh fights against the spirit and the only way we can please the Lord is in the spirit. The Holy Spirit is the Spirit of Truth and we must be filled with the Holy Spirit. He leads us to live in truth and not fall for lies, repent when we sin, and to be open and real before the Lord at all times. Do not pretend to be something you are not; God is all-knowing, so why bother hiding your true self. God can only shape and mold your true self, not a pretend version of yourself.

Notice the word *holy* in the above passages: holy God, holy place, and to present your bodies holy. God is holy and must be treated as such. By definition, holy means "exalted or worthy of complete devotion as one perfect in goodness and righteousness." In Revelation 4:8, we get a peek inside heaven;

"Each of the four living creatures had six wings and was covered with eyes all around, even under its wings. Day and night they never stop saying: "'Holy, holy, holy is the Lord God Almighty, who was, and is, and is to come." They cry holy *day and night.* Praise His holy name forever!

Worship to God must be performed in complete devotion to Him—not partial devotion and reserving some parts of our heart for sinful pleasures. True worship is an *all or nothing* act. We come into His presence with *fear* or *reverence*, and present our bodies as a living, holy sacrifice. The Bible says in 1 Peter 1:16, "Be holy, for I am holy." In other words, what we do in our bodies affects our spirit. When we sin, and fail to repent, a pure heart becomes impure.

Sin in our lives and the works of the flesh are: adultery, fornication, uncleanness, lasciviousness, idolatry, witchcraft, hatred, variance, emulations, wrath, strife, seditions, heresies, envyings, murders, drunkenness, and revelings—and cannot stand in the presence of a holy God. We must repent, and God is quick to forgive and restore (the baptism of the Holy Spirit helps in this sanctification process).

Instead, what pleases the Lord is when the fruit of the spirit characterize us: love, joy, peace, longsuffering, gentleness, goodness, faithfulness, meekness (submissiveness), and temperance. We don't talk about temperance much; however, its definition is powerful: "Temperance is a Bible word that every Bible Christian should know. It is the Spirit-empowered ability to control appetites, emotions, and attitudes. It is the capacity to resist sin" (paulechapman.com).

Now you can see how true worship is a lifestyle: while the world is dominated by hate, we love; when depression and doom is the new normal, we have joy; when chaos and rumors of war are heard, we have peace; when the world is impatient, we are longsuffering; when the world is cruel and harsh, we are gentle; as the world becomes more wicked and evil, we are full of God's goodness; when the world is full of doubt and unbelief, we are full of faith; while the world is rebellious toward God and toward law and order, we are submitted to God and submitted to law and order. Do not conform to the ways of this world in thoughts or in actions—God's ways are different, God's ways are higher, and God's ways are perfect!

Praise and worship time in a church service is a spiritual act, in a holy place, not a common place—like a sports arena or music hall (certainly these places can be converted into a church or holy place). Our spiritual worship includes the following: bringing an offering, using our lips and voices to sing, lifting holy hands, bowing in worship (even to our knees), dancing with our legs, and incorporating musical instruments (skillfully played; otherwise, it is a disturbance)—all to express what is happening on the inside, in the heart.

As we see in 1 Timothy 2:8, worship that is pleasing to God includes having love in your heart, and forgiving those who have hurt you, even if you think they don't deserve forgiveness. It also includes having full faith that what you are doing and saying—matters.

The object of our worship is Jesus. The songs that we sing, the lyrics, should be expressions of who God is, His love, His salvation, His mighty works, His plans for us, and His goodness. Lyrics straight from scripture are effective in ushering in the presence of God. Songs open up the windows of the heart (for good or for evil). Worship that is pleasing to God is only when He is at the center, His name is glorified; and all flesh must die or humble itself in His presence. When this happens, the Holy Spirit has full reign—full reign to heal, to save, and to perform miracles for His glory.

The *worship team* in a church is a significant element of worship—a deal breaker if you will. It can be an *obstacle* or a launching pad into the presence of God. The first thing humans look for is talent—can you sing or play an instrument. Talent is important and without it, a person can be a distraction and a hindrance in a worship service, which is not what we want. But the most important aspect of a worship leader is *the heart of the worship leader.* You are leading the church into the holy of holies; and in order to do so, you must also be holy, submitted and completely devoted to the Lord in every area of your life. If you want to enter into the presence of God, this is key. This doesn't mean you are perfect yet; it means you are submitted and God has the steering wheel, while you are learning to stay humble and follow His lead.

Furthermore, you cannot confidently lead others into places you have not been before. What does your one-on-one worship time with the Lord look like? God's presence can be felt daily. The more time you spend with the Holy Spirit, the better you will know Him, and He will show you how to lead others into God's presence.

Together, as one church body, we must worship in spirit and in truth. No flesh can glory in God's presence. If a worship leader or team is worshipping in the flesh and bringing glory to flesh, this is idolatry, setting yourself above God and provoking God to anger (Deuteronomy 4). Our praises must lift up the name of Jesus and no one else, including self.

Strange Fire

I visited a large, local modern church for their Wednesday evening services, for a couple of months. I was invited by a friend, and I was so looking forward to worshipping my heart out— singing, clapping, shouting, lifting my hands in praise, and not sticking out like a sore thumb being one of a few people doing so. So I did just that.

I entered the church early and found a seat. The church was already pretty full with many lovely, happy people. Once worship was about to start, the lights went dim, and colorful lights also appeared. A worship leader and a team of about ten others took the stage. I closed my eyes and pretty much worshipped the entire time with my eyes shut. I knew all the songs and didn't even need to look at the projected words. I worshipped freely. It was awesome!

Next came some announcements, and the message preached by the senior pastor, which I thought was a solid message.

I went home after service all excited to tell my husband about how wonderful this church was. They also were well equipped with a children's church program and nursery care, which would meet the needs of our young family, and allow us adults to participate in church services. I suggested we visit the church on a Sunday with the family and try it out to see if we all liked it.

I went to sleep that night, and woke up probably four or five times during the night in severe panic. I felt like I was in some kind of spiritual battle—a demonic one. That entire night was rough. The next morning and during the next day, I thought about my nightmares from the previous night. I had no explanation. I went to church happy, came home happy, and went to sleep to be attacked by demons. Weird.

I continued to go to this church's midweek service for several weeks. On the second week's visit, I kept my eyes mostly open, rather than closed, during worship. I wanted to observe the worship service. The songs were biblically based and reflected God's character. The worship team appeared to be spiritual and humble, modestly dressed—not trying to draw attention to themselves by the clothes they were wearing, or lack thereof, nor with their body language or body movements.

But the worship leader, I'm sorry to say, was all flesh. It was like a performance at an arts theatre or something. One could easily forget they are in a church service and think they are watching the lead actress perform at a Broadway show. It was all about her!

How evil in the sight of God! Man must become small, humble herself and himself, so that God can show up mighty. If flesh is dominating the stage, this leaves no room for the Holy Spirit.

This is idolatry, placing yourself above God, which stirs the anger of God. Idolatry is in the same category of other big sins. Certainly, all sins separate us from God, however, we humans have a way of magnifying certain sins and minimizing others. We read in 1 Corinthians 6: 9–10, "Do you not know that the wicked will not inherit the kingdom of God? Do not be deceived:

Neither the sexually immoral nor idolaters nor adulterers nor male prostitutes nor homosexual offenders nor thieves nor the greedy nor drunkards nor slanderers nor swindlers will inherit the kingdom of God."

On the contrary, worship leaders are to be full of the Holy Spirit and led by the Spirit. Psalm 40:3 says, "He put a new song in my mouth, a song of praise to our God. Many will see and fear, and put their trust in the Lord." This is the biblical example of what a godly worship leader should look like. The words coming out of your mouth, words from the Spirit, will cause people to have holy fear of God and cause them to trust the Lord. Praise God!

This glory of the flesh, or anything that would rob from God's glory, has no place in God's house! This behavior begs the question, "How does the senior pastor, who is ultimately responsible for all activities going on in church, not see this ballad?" The worship was clearly being tainted by the worship leader.

Discerning what is happening—inside the church, outside the church, in your own personal life and family—takes the filling or baptism of the Holy Spirit and practice. In time, through testing of different circumstances you will walk through, you will learn to discern truth from lies and good from evil.

This experience I had reminded me of the story in Leviticus about *burning strange fire;* "Nadab and Abihu were killed because of their disregard for the utter holiness of God and the need to

126

honor and obey Him in solemn and holy fear. Their carelessness and irreverence were their downfall" (gotquestions.org).

I believe when I was worshiping, blindly...literally, I was partaking in this strange fire, which I believe explains the nightmares I had that night after the first service. I went into this church trusting that all that was to take place was of God. I made assumptions, we all do, and this is not a good thing. We must search for truth, not assume a position and treat it as truth.

So is this church I referenced going to hell, with all of its members? Absolutely not; however, changes must occur. The baptism of the Holy Spirit must be taught, desired, asked for, and received by every member and leader in Jesus' name. The Holy Spirit will guide the church in all truth. This is a promise from God our Father.

Why is it so dark in here?

So we have looked at scriptural praise and worship, but what about style of worship? Every church is different. What does God desire? God desires unity and love among His members. John 17:21 says, "I pray that they will all be one, just as you and I are one—as you are in me, Father, and I am in you. And may they be in us so that the world will believe you sent me." Right now there is a huge divide. How do we become one? We must become one *before* Christ's return—so that the world will see, so that the world will believe, in Jesus Christ.

My parents are from the old country, as my dad would proudly put it, and conservation is one of their key priorities. In our home,food was never wasted,and money was not spent frivolously. Lights were turned on when absolutely necessary; if you walked out of a room and the light remained on, someone had some major explaining to do.

From the age of five until I got married, I lived in this cozy conservative ranch. Only after I moved out, and then came to visit my parents, did I notice the following. I would walk in the house (morning, noon, or evening) and often wonder and even say, "Why is it so dark in here?" My mom looked at me like I was speaking a foreign language, and I guess I was. When I lived at home, the lighting in the house went unnoticed. After living in my own home with my husband, large modern windows with so much natural light passing through became my new normal. Had I continued to live in my parents' house until I was forty years old, it probably would have never occurred to me how dark the entire house was.

This realization has helped me understand and hopefully explain accurately the atmosphere in modern-day worship services. If a first-time visitor were to walk into most church services today, right before worship service starts, they would experience the lights going dim. "Why is it so dark in here? Is it nap time?" Then the stage lights turn on, there is the presence or absence of a smoke machine, and there is a stage where one key singer (worship leader) is joined by other singers and musicians. Now I'm thinking, "This is pretty cool...just like being at a concert." I wait for the entertainment to start.

If you are a believer in the age bracket of teens to thirties, this type of worship is all you know about worship services; and therefore, it is normal, and it must also be godly, right? What else would it be if it isn't godly? After all, I'm in church. It would take someone from the outside, someone who has had a different worship experience to come in and say, "Can we make this better?"

I never attended a non-Christian concert, even though I lived in the world for a period of time during my teen years. However, I am aware of secular artists. So I jumped on YouTube and searched for an artist almost everyone knows, Michael Jackson. He was performing on stage, in concert. Guess what I saw? Dim auditorium, smoke, stage lights, one person—Michael Jackson—dressed in a shiny outfit. The audience was praising him, very literally, and some were even fainting. Where did the world get the idea of creating this dark atmosphere, filled with smoke? Without further research, sounds like hell, right? Remember, Satan was a worshiper of God in heaven, where only light exists. However, he rebelled and was thrown down into darkness. He knew what worship in heaven looked like; however, we know that Satan takes truth and distorts it, even doing the exact opposite.

I searched for any indication in the Bible—to see if it was or is ever dark in heaven during worship to God. This seems even silly to consider, darkness in heaven? Never! Nonetheless, I wanted to cover my bases, and uncovered the following from scripture.

God himself is light; therefore, darkness cannot exist in His presence. His very being is like the brightness of the sun. Worshipers surround the throne, worshiping continually. Therefore, it is very bright in heaven during worship.

All over scripture, beginning with Genesis, God, Jesus, and the Holy Spirit represent light; "In the beginning God created the heavens and the earth. Now the earth was formless and empty, darkness was over the surface of the deep, and the Spirit of God was hovering over the waters. And God said, 'Let there be light,' and there was light. God saw that the light was good, and he separated the light from the darkness" (Genesis 1:1–4). Furthermore, in John 8:12, we read, "When Jesus spoke again to the people, he said, 'I am the light of the world. Whoever follows me will never walk in darkness, but will have the light of life." There are probably hundreds of references you can find yourself where *light* is tied to the Trinity and *dark* is linked to the devil.

Some of these references about light are literal and some are metaphorical; still, how did we go the opposite way and turn our worship services into dark sanctuaries?

Notice that Michael Jackson, as well as Elvis Presley and others, started off as church singers—in the days of sanctuaries with beautiful windows, natural light, well-lit services, and no smoke machines.

I think we can all agree that the Michael Jackson concert atmosphere is worldly, and this depiction is strikingly similar to Christian concerts, and runs parallel with some modern worship services. Not all, but at least some of what is taking place in our worship services is *worldly.*

The result of these *mixed signals* in worship services is confusion. Believe it or not, the world expects the church to be different. My best guess as to why modern-day Christian worship services resemble this Michael Jackson concert is because we have imitated the world (and we don't even realize it). When the church imitates the world, it dishonors God.

Who does the Bible tell us to imitate? "Be imitators of God" (Ephesians 5:1). Additionally, Romans 12:2 reads, "Do not be conformed to this world..." Christian churches do themselves a disservice when they imitate the world. This world portrays a dark room, light show, smoke, and worship of man. We have tried to make people feel comfortable, with an inviting atmosphere, something they can relate to—like being at a rock concert. However, people come to church because they are searching for something different, something that is missing, something they searched for but did not find in worldly pleasures. *Capitalize on that* and fill the internal void with the truth from the Word of God. What will set people free? The truth will set people free (John 8:32). All the distractions—light show, smoke, excessive loudness—are distracting.

Does this mean these churches with their members are going to hell? Absolutely not! However, some analysis and changes need to take place. Worship must resemble God and heaven, not the devil and the world. I know times change; and as long as things change for the better, meaning the changes are drawing us closer to God and into the presence of God, then awesome—keep them coming. But if changes are taking the focus off of God and placing it on man (or anything else but God), this should be our red flag to stop and evaluate our works.

Working or just chillin'

How far will the church go to please God? If worldly worship appeases people and this flesh nature, then godly worship should have God as its center and worship of Him only. An experience at church should be an experience of worship, not an experience of entertainment. One churchgoer interviewed for a television special said he wished his church services were longer because they were like "a good movie" (equip.org). How can you ensure you are worshiping and not just being entertained?

Worship is giving; entertainment is receiving.

Worship is joining in; entertainment is remaining a spectator.

Worship requires effort; entertainment requires zero effort.

The kingdom of God is just the reverse or opposite of entertainment. *I am doing something*: singing, clapping, dancing, raising holy hands, praying, reading the Bible, fasting, increasing my faith, helping the poor, laying hands on the sick, casting out demons, teaching the Bible to my children (even caring for our childrens' earthly needs is works for the kingdom), spreading the Gospel, visiting the sick, or sharing words of encouragement—for example. I am doing all of these good works as an act of worship to God.

Do you see how much work needs to be done? If we get distracted, caught up with self and this world, we fail, and the devil wins. We read in 2 Timothy 3:1–3, "But understand this: In the last days terrible times will come. For men will be lovers of themselves, lovers of money, boastful, arrogant, abusive, disobedient to their parents, ungrateful, unholy, unloving, unforgiving, slanderous, without self-control, brutal, without love of good." Let us be about our Father's business, working for Him, being filled with the Spirit, leaving no room for the works of the flesh.

We know the devil's plan is to stop God's plan. One of the tools the devil is using is entertainment. What I wish I knew even sooner is the fact that children's cartoons, TV shows, movies, even youtube for kids—are sprinkled with sin and garbage (because the hearts of the producers and CEOs of these companies are *of this world*). It is time for us to pray for the salvation of men and women in high ranking positions. Once their hearts are changed, their work will also change, for the good. Furthermore, Christians with financial wealth must rise up, and produce God-filtered, great entertainment and video games. Whatever the case (Christian or secular), we must *always* be careful, be cautious (but not overly cautious, for this will cause anxiety), and be vigilant; monitoring what our children are watching, playing, and discussing among themselves. TVs and monitors in an open space, like the living room (not bedroom), help in doing so. This very action *encourages* children and adults to be conscious, aware, and accountable for what they see, hear, and speak. Teach your children what is wholesome, what is godly, and this training (discern good from evil and choose good) will remain with your children forever.

Certainly, the devil doesn't want us doing God's work—reading and sharing the Word, praying, singing, etc. So he takes our eyes off the real prize—eternal bliss with our Savior Jesus Christ—and shifts them to fruitless things. This is very easy to do, since entertainment requires zero effort on our part. Working out is hard; sitting on the couch is easy. Following a diet to lose body fat is hard; eating whatever I crave is easy. You get the idea.

Via entertainment, we have been trained to sit back and wait for something to happen. What does the Bible say? Are we to sit and hope or hope and act? Consider this example of how faith (the substance of things hoped for) is directly linked to works (actions):

> But do you want to know, O foolish man, that faith without works is dead? Was not Abraham our father justified by works when he offered Isaac his son on the altar? Do you see that faith was working together with his works, and by works faith was made perfect? And the Scripture was fulfilled which says, "Abraham believed God, and it was accounted to him for righteousness." And he was called the friend of God. You see then that a man is justified by works, and not by faith only. Likewise, was not Rahab the harlot also

> justified by works when she received the
> messengers and sent them out another way?
> For as the body without the spirit is dead,
> so faith without works is dead also.
> (James 2:20–26)

God does not want us to be lazy. He wants us to act. Notice that all of these items are verbs—action words: singing, clapping, dancing, raising holy hands, praying, reading the Bible, fasting, etc. This isn't a religious list of things you do to receive salvation from God. He loves you regardless. However, in His kingdom, there is movement and work taking place—no spectators here! Watching movies or football games, and any screen time, are not bad in themselves. However, the American society, and probably global society, has become an entertainment glutton. Right now I have a mental image of Jabba the Hutt, who is "a fictional character in the Star Wars franchise created by George Lucas. He is a large, slug-like alien known as a Hutt" (wikipedia.com). Even being full of church sermons for years and years, yet never giving away or spreading the message of Christ to others, is unhealthy.

We were created for work. My dad was right, although he could use an adjustment to his eighty-hour Romanian workweek. To want to do something productive and meaningful, and to have a purpose, are all God-implanted attributes.

Jesus talks about the lazy steward and his reward. But he also talks about the faithful steward. What does the Bible say of his or her reward? "The Lord said, 'Who then is the faithful and wise steward [of the estate], whom his master will put in charge over his household, to give his servants their portion of food at the proper time? Blessed (happy, prosperous, to be admired) is that servant whom his master finds so doing when he arrives. I assure you and most solemnly say to you, he will put him in charge of all his possessions'" (Luke 12: 42-44). Be faithful with all God's given you—gifts, talents, family, and career—and He will promote you, as only He can.

All gifts—to preach or sing, the power to get wealth, the beauty you possess—are gifts from God to be used for glorifying Him. You cannot take credit for these gifts. When man takes credit for something God gave or did, this is an abomination. Be careful—this can happen in our churches as well and in the daily lives of Christians. Read your Bible daily to stay humble— remaining in truth, filled with the Holy Spirit. If someone pays you a compliment, pass it forward, up to the King of kings and Lord of lords, where all good things come from. Without Him, we are barren; yet, in His hands, we are fruitful. Hallelujah!

Since his fall, the devil has tried to take credit from God and distort God's plan. The devil took his eyes off of God and placed them on self; thus, the object of the devil's worship became self; and he wants you to do the same. With our gifts and talents, we must stay far away from pride. People caught in pride don't realize they are serving the devil. However, there are only two masters— God and Satan. One chooses through their actions whom they will serve. There is no middle ground, as the devil would have people believe. As pride grows, the prideful person is left believing that there is no one like himself or herself. Don't allow pride (or any other sin) to creep in—remain in obedience to the Word of God.

When Jesus was tempted by the devil, the third and final temptation was the promise of having all the kingdoms in the world, if only Jesus would fall and worship him—that's how important worship is. Remain a true worshiper. Worship God only, not self or this world. Worship the Lord in Spirit and in truth!

Chapter 6

In the World, but Not of the World

If you are reading this book, you were born into this world. From the time God created the heavens and the earth, billions of people came the same way; there is no choice in the matter. We exist in the world, and our human nature is of this world.

What we do have control over, or a choice about, is if we will continue to be of this world, or choose to be part of God's world or God's kingdom.

Once we are saved and receive the Spirit of God, we join God's family. We are no longer of this world—our zip code changed, and our thinking must also change. Jesus spent much time teaching in parables, trying to portray and help people understand that there is another kingdom, the kingdom of God, and that it was not of this world. It had completely different attributes and different characteristics.

In fact, God's kingdom is directly opposite the world and its ways. The world teaches that there is no absolute truth, and to live in the moment, doing whatever feels good—the Word instructs in Titus 2: 11–12, "For the grace of God has appeared that offers salvation to all people. It teaches us to say "No" to ungodliness and worldly passions, and to live self-controlled, upright and godly lives in this present age." The world also says, "Who knows if there is life after death anyway?" The truth is, this earthly life is temporary—a drop in a bucket. Heaven or hell is forever. We read in 1 John 2:17, "The world and its desires pass away, but whoever does the will of God lives forever."

One may think, can I be in this world, be of this world, and of God's kingdom too? James 4:4 says, "You adulterous people, don't you know that friendship with the world means enmity against God? Therefore, anyone who chooses to be a friend of the world becomes an enemy of God." The good news is that with the spirit of God on the inside, we overcome the world (1 John 5:4); and the work that God started, He will finish(Philippians 1:6).

The Bible tells us not to conform to the things of this world, but rather to be *transformed* by the renewing of the mind. We see this in Romans 12:2; "Don't copy the behavior and customs of this world, but let God transform you into a new person by changing the way you think. Then you will learn to know God's will for you, which is good and pleasing and perfect."

So changing the way you think leads to you being a new person, or having *new thoughts equals a new person.* This new person can be entrusted to make good, sound judgments and decisions. These Holy Spirit-led decisions will affect you and your family for the good; they will lead to pleasing and wonderful things happening in your life and the lives of those around you.

Christians often think and ask, "What is God's will for my life?" The answer is found here in Romans 12:2. When God transforms your thinking, you will learn to know God's will for you.

As we grow in Christ (and are transformed through a renewed mind), we become less like the natural man, and more like the spiritual man, having the mind of Christ:

> The natural man does not accept the things that come from the Spirit of God. For they are foolishness to him, and he cannot understand them, because they are spiritually discerned. The spiritual man judges all things, but he himself is not subject to anyone's judgement. "For who has known the mind of the Lord, so as to instruct Him?" But we have the mind of Christ..." (1 Corinthians 2:14–16)

Essentially, this new mind is the mind of Christ, and it gives us the capability to understand spiritual things. Our job is to renew our minds with the washing of the Word of God and search for truth (not assume a position and treat it as truth); and once we find truth, hold on to it, and live by it. The Holy Spirit, or the Spirit of Truth, helps in doing so.

Consequently, if we do not obey what we already know to be true, it will be evident in our daily lives, expressed through frustration and unrest. This spiritual stand-still, or spiritual decline really, can be avoided if we obey truth when it is revealed to us. Only then can we move forward in our relationship with Christ.

As I'm working on this chapter, I'm wondering, why didn't God just download new thoughts into our heads the moment we got saved? Perhaps some people think He did, or thought He did, before looking closer at these passages. Notice Apostle Paul's writings (a good portion of the New Testament), and how many instructions he provided to believers through his letters and in person, as he traveled to the different cities and churches. If we received a new mind (the mind of Christ) at the same time as receiving salvation (or water baptism or the baptism of the Holy Spirit), there wouldn't have been a need for Paul to pour out his heart in all of those letters—giving instructions on how to live a pure and holy life unto the Lord.

I believe the answer, to why God didn't just give us a new mind, lies in a couple of reasons. First, God never wanted robots. He created us with free will, and the freedom of choice.

He never uses force, control, or manipulation. He desires that we choose Him, choose life, choose righteousness—but God forces no one. Secondly, the reason why God didn't just give us new minds is that God desires to have a personal relationship, a close friendship, with each person. The very reason we were created is for fellowship, or companionship, with our Creator. As we get to know His ways, and obey His ways; a devoted, loving relationship forms and grows between you and God—until you are one with Him. The entire body of Christ, or the bride of Christ, is meant to be one with her groom, Jesus Christ.

To summarize the topic of *the mind of Christ,* when we get saved, our spirit becomes alive for Christ, but our mind is the same. When we spend time with the Lord—time in prayer, time in the Bible, time in fasting, and time with other believers—our thinking and actions change. Over time, we develop the mind of Christ.

If you capture a person's mind, you can easily capture their heart. There is a real battle for your heart! Whoever owns your heart, owns you, and owns your eternity. Therefore, guard your heart. Let's read what Proverbs 4: 23-27 has to say about the heart, the mouth, the eyes, and the feet:

> Above all else, guard your heart, for
> everything you do flows from it.
>
> Keep your mouth free of perversity; keep
> corrupt talk far from your lips.

143

Let your eyes look straight ahead;
fix your gaze directly before you.

Give careful thought to the paths for your feet
and be steadfast in all your ways.

Do not turn to the right or the left;
keep your foot from evil.

How do you guard your heart (and stay far from sin)? By loving what God loves, and hating what God hates; therefore not allowing those things that God hates into your heart. Mind what you see and hear, what your thoughts are, and mind your actions done in this human body—ensuring they are all pleasing to the Lord. And when they are not, be quick to ask forgiveness of the Father, and turn from it.

What do you seek?

This entire book is designed to present truth from the Bible, and if need-be, change your thoughts—ensuring that your thoughts and my thoughts are based on truth found in God's Word. These thoughts will lead to actions, actions lining up with the will of God—specifically for the days we are living now. One of the questions I'd like us to ask ourselves is,"What am I seeking?" Specifically, what do you seek for yourself, your spouse, and your children? It is evident what someone is seeking by how they spend their time, how they spend their money, and what they talk about. Matthew 6:21 says, "For where your treasure is, there your heart will be also."

If your emphasis is on this life—your career, your kids' career, your positions, your possessions—your heart will also be tied to this life. God wants our hearts tied to Him, and you do too. How do we get there?

First, realize that God is all-knowing, all-sovereign, and all-loving toward you. He wants your best, and knows what's best for you. But you have to learn to trust Him. Matthew 6: 31–33 says, "Therefore do not be anxious, saying, 'What shall we eat?' or 'What shall we drink?' or 'What shall we wear?' For the Gentiles seek after all these things, and your heavenly Father knows that you need them all. But seek first the kingdom of God and his righteousness, and all these things will be added to you."

The world says, "Get a good education, compete for the finest schools and top professions, obtain a great paying job, acquire an esteemed position, and provide an abundance of things for yourself and for your family." *God says* to seek His kingdom and His righteousness first, and after you do so, all these things will be added to you, or God will give them to you automatically. You don't have to chase them down so hard;

God will lead you to a great profession, with great pay, and give you the desire of your heart—*after* you make His kingdom your top priority.

You can answer for yourself if God's kingdom is first in your life. The fruit of a life surrendered unto the Lord, God being the top priority, is evident in: our love for others, our concern and outreach for the lost, our worship, and in our praise. If you discovered through self-analysis that in fact the kingdom of God is not first in your life, you can change today.

So how can I change and make God's kingdom my top priority? By making your relationship with God the number one priority in your life. All those around you will know when this happens—it is unmistakable.

After you get baptized or filled with the Spirit, you must be refilled daily. How? Through prayer, I ask God to fill me daily; and I also take some actions, that you can try also. First, cut back on the noise, or turn it off altogether, until you get your thinking straight (social media, tv programs, busy schedules). This isn't about being legalistic, but rather these are tips on how to know what's deeper. Multitasking is oftentimes unavoidable; however, to seek God and hear him clearly, it needs to be quiet—quiet literally (like when you are lying in bed at night) and quiet in your spirit (cast out all fear in Jesus' name). In the quiet, in the silence, while you are still—the Holy Spirit will show you what is fruitful and unfruitful in your life.

Furthermore, be mindful of your actions daily. What we set before our eyes and ears can either build us up or tear us down—by introducing sin through godless ideas. Am I saying it's bad to watch TV and movies, and visit YouTube and Facebook? No. These things aren't wrong if they don't dominate your life (keep you from working or taking care of your family), don't keep you from doing works for God, don't lure you into temptation and sin, and don't taint (contaminate or pollute) your conscience.

We must design our daily schedule on purpose to put kingdom priorities first—time in prayer, time in the Word, time in helping others. Let's ensure that what we do doesn't grieve the heart of God; meaning, we refrain from evil at all costs. Lord give us strength!

My Christianity determines what I set before my eyes and ears—my flesh does not. The flesh will lead you astray, and the flesh must be crucified. Our thoughts must be changed so that we can make good choices about what we set before our eyes and ears, how we spend our time, and what we do in these earthly bodies.

The Temple of the Holy Spirit

Your body is the temple of the Holy Spirit, or the Spirit of God resides in you; "Do you not know that your body is a temple of the Holy Spirit who is in you, whom you have received from

God? You are not your own; you were bought at a price. Therefore glorify God with your body" (1 Corinthians 6: 19–20). Your body should be holy in every aspect—in speech, in thoughts, in actions, in what I view and listen to, and in how I dress.

Perhaps you are a person reading this, and thinking, "Why even discuss such topics? Aren't we saved by grace?" Yes, we are saved by grace; "For by grace you have been saved through faith" (Eph. 2:8). However, faith without works is dead (James 2:17), therefore our works (actions performed in this human body)—matter. These topics are important to understand and implement for our personal sanctification and for unity in the entire body of Christ. Jesus will return for a bride dressed in white; without spot, blemish or wrinkle—united in love. Let's tear down the walls of division by uniting around the truth found in God's Word and live in obedience to the entire Bible.

First, let's look at the woman's temple; "Likewise, I want the women to adorn themselves with respectable apparel, with modesty, and with self-control, not with braided hair or gold or pearls or expensive clothes, but with good deeds, appropriate for women who profess to worship God" (1 Timothy 2:9). *Adorn* by definition means to make more beautiful or attractive. In God's kingdom, women are allowed to make themselves more beautiful, modestly, however their true beauty comes from their good works or inner self.

Furthermore, *Modesty* defined is being free from vanity, egotism, boastfulness, or great pretensions and *respectable* means being regarded by society to be good, proper, or correct (www.dictionary.com). A synonym for *self-control* is self-restraint—and the opposite of control is to indulge.

Dressing for church or for anywhere else should be respectable and modest. You do not belong to yourself, you belong to God, and His Word tells us to dress respectably and modestly, with self-control.

Ask yourself when you shop, "Who am I trying to please?" We should be aiming to please God; "For the fruit of the light consists in all goodness, righteousness, and truth. *Test and prove what pleases the Lord.* Have no fellowship with the fruitless deeds of darkness, but rather expose them" (Ephesians 5:9–11).

You can and should ask the Holy Spirit to teach you how to dress modestly. Modesty to me means I am not trying to boast about or display how wealthy I am, how fit I am, or how fashionable I am—with my outer apparel (clothing, jewelry, hair, and make-up). If you are *of this world,* you focus on self and edify self. However, for the Christian, the attention should be shifted off of self and onto Christ—edifying and uplifting Christ in all things. When the world sees us, they should see Christ. Ultimately, modesty is a heart issue. When you know who you are in Christ—that you are loved beyond measure and complete in Him—modesty will come naturally. The need to show others your pros (advantages, assets) will disappear.

Leggings, skinny jeans, short shorts, short skirts, low cut tops, tight clothes, belly shirts, and tight dresses—are all immodest, unrespectable, and without self-control (not to mention a huge temptation for men). Men are visual (by God's design) and are automatically attracted to a nice-looking body. Just like a man can easily take advantage of a woman's emotions (her vulnerability); women, when you dress in these ways, you are taking advantage of men's vulnerabilities (intentionally or unintentionally). For this reason, the female body must be covered appropriately. You don't want to invite negative attention from men—attention that very well could lead to sin. Nor do you want to cause someone to stumble, due to how much of your body you are revealing. Dress modestly, dress respectably, and dress with self-control—thereby not tempting men of any age (in church and in the outside world). Women want to be treated equal to men, not treated like an object of sorts. Here's your chance—dress godly.

If you are a man reading this and find yourself dominated (to look once is normal, to look twice is sin) by lust and what your eyes see, go talk to your pastor. The only way lust will be removed is through confession and the blood of Jesus. The chains can be broken, in the name of Jesus, and you can live a life that is set-free from all addictions.

In marriage, in the bedroom, is where it is God's plan for a woman to reveal her curves—to her husband only.

Some women dress immodestly because they haven't been taught differently; it is the cultural norm today to wear leggings…everywhere…for example. When I was growing up, something similar to leggings was worn. However, it was worn underneath a long sweater that more than covered your bottom. Today, little girls, teenagers, and grown women wear leggings as their lower garment or instead of pants. Leggings are hardly thicker than stockings, and if anyone hasn't noticed, leggings show off everything—whether you are in shape or not. Your body should never be revealed in such a way in public. The fashion industry managed to sell a $2 piece of cloth for $20. Some cost more than $100, and apparently they have leggings for work too. Hmmm, I wonder how different those are from the leggings you wear to school, to the gym, or to bed for that matter.

Some women purposely dress immodestly to attract other men. What such women don't realize is that they are luring a man's flesh, not capturing his heart necessarily, nor moving toward a lasting marriage relationship. If you can turn his head so easily, so can hundreds of other women.

I'd love to see some awesome, talented, Holy Spirit-filled women open up their own fashion lines—beautiful, modest, elegant clothing for women (including wedding dresses). Christians can change the fashion trends—changes that can revolutionize America and the globe.

Women should be characterized by what's beneath the outer beauty. Women of God must be known first and foremost for their character that reflects Christ—a lifestyle of good works. Spend more time on improving your character, rather than over-focusing on your aging body. We read in 1 Timothy 4:8, "For physical training is of some value, but godliness has value for all things, holding promise for both the present life and the life to come." Christians should certainly engage in some sort of resistance training, some physical activity, on a regular basis. But this, or any earthly occupation or hobby—should never define us, nor supersede our main objective, of being servants to Christ.

Furthermore, Proverbs explains, "Charm is deceptive, and beauty does not last; but a woman who fears the LORD will be greatly praised" (Proverbs 31:30). The sooner we grab a hold of this verse, the better. What will bring you true happiness and peace is doing the will of the Lord. No amount of plastic surgery, botox, fake eyelashes, or heavy make-up—will bring you happiness, or a better marriage, or a better man.

Here is what some men of different ages and backgrounds and of no particular religious affiliation had said about fake lashes and makeup (from Get the Gloss):

Question: *"When it comes to your makeup, what do men actually want?"*

Answers: *"Fresh face, less is more, makeup that highlights natural beauty & enhancement of features; anything fake e.g., eyelashes, looks scary, and anything with glitter is irritating because it gets everywhere."*

Ladies, you've heard it from the men—less is more, and natural is key!

Now, let's talk about the man's temple. Somehow, not sure how, the fashion industry has been successful in selling and making popular skinny jeans and skinny pants for boys and men. How did they manage to sell this successfully? Pants so tight that your body parts can't breathe, relax, or feel any comfort. Weird, right? I learned in school that in order for a man to have healthy sperm, the male scrotum is to remain away from the body to ensure it has a cooler temperature than the rest of the body. Clearly, skinny jeans do just the opposite. I encourage men and boys to buy clothes that are comfortable. Don't allow the fashion industry, who is hungry for profits, to tell you what you should be wearing.

Most women prefer a manly man, and I'm pretty sure that doesn't include skinny jeans. Godly women looking for a real, meaningful relationship that will lead to marriage are most interested in your character—how you treat her, how you treat others, how you love God, and not in your curves.

Through constant advertising, the fashion industry has shaped our thinking, thus controlling our actions—*when the true words in the Bible* and *common sense*—should be shaping our thinking and controlling our actions.

In God's kingdom, modesty must be upheld. Biblical principles taught in churches will lead to holiness in the entire body of Christ. My actions affect the entire body, and we must all do our part—live holy unto the Lord.

Remember, we are in this world, yet not of this world. When your focus is eternity and doing God's will—this body, this life, is not that important. Aging and death are inevitable. Do your best to eat, sleep, exercise, and relax your mind and body—appropriately and in a healthy way. Those are the things you *can* control. The rest is in God's hands. Your personal value and self-worth should not be tied to things that are here today and pass away tomorrow. Find your value in Christ—He remains forever!

Music

Whatever you feed, grows; and what people don't always realize is that *music* has a big impact on our thoughts, actions, and emotions.

For example, if you often listen to sad, sappy love songs, you will become a sad sap for love. It will be all you long for, all you think about. This is a terrible way to live, for a man or woman cannot solve your happiness problem.

Or if I listen to songs that talk about women as being b**ches and h***, then I will begin to view the women around me in that same way, and treat them as such, with disrespect.

If I repeatedly sing a song about getting lucky tonight…come on, you get the picture.

When you listen to an artist that you enjoy, you are opening your heart wide open to that person and what they are saying; you are joining in, partaking. You have *unguarded* your heart, and you didn't even know it, and there are consequences to doing so. Likewise, singing worship songs *that you enjoy* opens up your heart to the Holy Spirit and godly things.

I google artists and authors, to find out who they are, what they are about, before I go any further—for both Christians and non-Christians. I suggest you do the same. You don't want to open your heart up to strange things. Even music that seems harmless—

no dirty language; just happy, upbeat, mystical music—be careful about. Google the artist. He or she could very well be into new-age garbage that you want no part of as a Christian. Research them, research their work, to find out who they truly are.

Some music is clearly *of this world* and all Christians should have no part in music performed by secular artists such as Lady Gaga, Beyonce, and Katy Perry (to name a few). There are many others out there. Do your own research on your favorite artists. What you will find will be shocking. Read the lyrics. The artists I mentioned here are involved in demonic activity and drinking human blood, research showed. One source says, "In the real, modern world, famous people sell their souls to the devil for the magic to make millions of dollars selling generic pop music" (www.theatlantic.com). I am not trying to be legalistic here, just presenting information to help you clear out those things that are hurting your relationship with Christ, and those things detestable in the sight of God. These things, *the things of this world*, ought to be detestable to us, too.

I personally stick to Christian music, Christian music stations, and even am careful with these. One Christian artist was on the Ellen DeGeneres Show and was asked by a reporter sometime thereafter if homosexuality is a sin. She couldn't say, "Yes, homosexuality is a sin. That is what the Bible says." Perhaps she was catering to her new friend and the fame that comes with it. Or perhaps she doesn't know that homosexuality is a sin. I don't know the answer, God knows; however, if Christians don't represent Christ and the truth in the Bible, who will? We must read our Bible, understand our Bible (read the version you understand, otherwise you will not be able to apply what you've read), live the truth ourselves, then speak the truth in love. This is Christianity in a nutshell. Lord help us! The Lord *is* helping us and will help us—through His Holy Spirit.

From the day I got saved at the age of 18, I banned all secular music stations. I changed the settings in my car, and I threw out all non-christian CD's. If you are honest with yourself, you will agree that the music, the talk, the conversations on secular stations are ungodly and unfruitful. I encourage you to "rip the band-aid off" as I did. You may not have CD's, but you have playlists, and on demand lists, and favorite series on Netflix— that need a second look. Those things displeasing to God must go. If they stay, they will negatively affect your relationship with a holy God.

Leisure & enjoyment

One area that can be easily overlooked and misassessed, are those things we do for pleasure, leisure, or enjoyment: video games, favorite shows, different apps and social chat sites, and the like. Some will overlook their content and the impressions that they leave. However, whatever you engage in enters your mind (through your eyes and ears) and can easily enter your heart, especially if you are enjoying (or opening your heart to) what you are doing.

To be more specific, is a video game that engages the player in robbing banks, murdering people, adultery, pornography (including strip clubs), and using drugs and alcohol—*godly or worldly?* The answer is obvious—this is filth and sin at its finest—totally disgusting. Yet, some will make excuses, saying, "This is only a game." Not true. Jesus speaks in the gospels that even if you are *thinking* sin and don't actually commit sin with your body, it is still sin (Matthew 5).

Those things you write to someone via any chat are *real*, just like saying it in person, and should reflect your Christianity; "But the things that come out of the mouth come from the heart, and these things defile a man. For out of the heart come evil thoughts, murder, adultery, sexual immorality, theft, false testimony, and slander. These are what defile a man..." (Matthew 15:18–20).

How do these sins get into the heart? Through our eyes and ears information enters our mind, and we form thoughts—*good thoughts and bad thoughts*. Then thoughts travel to the heart. And when a person speaks, you find out what is in their heart.

We must cast down thoughts that don't line up with the scripture; "Casting down imaginations, and every high thing that exalts itself against the knowledge of God, and bringing into captivity every thought to the obedience of Christ..." (2 Corinthians 10:5). If you don't, the thought that sticks around will soon enter the heart. When something gets to the point that it enters your heart, it is a part of you, it is what you believe.

Thanks be to our holy God that the heart can be cleansed by the blood of Jesus, and we don't have to live worldly. *We can live godly!*

Are all games and social media apps bad? Not necessarily, however, being balanced is key, making your relationship with the Lord (through reading the Bible and praying) and your daily responsibilities—the priority. The more time you spend with God, the more your appetite for godly things will grow, and the desire for things that are fleeting and passing will diminish.

He Created Them Male and Female

Even though the answer is simple, and animals can figure it out instantly, the world today is questioning and second guessing the obvious or *the indisputable*. Genesis 5:1–2 says, "This is the book of the generations of Adam. In the day that God created man, He made him in His own likeness. *Male and female He created them*, and He blessed them." Who would have thought, even five years ago, that this scripture would be so relevant in the public school system and in the world we live in? Seeds have been planted of, "What gender am I?" I never thought this would even come up in conversation *as a joke*. Sadly, this is no joke. We are living in the last days.

I guess we shouldn't be too surprised. The devil wants to take everything that God made, which was made perfect, and distort it. He not only causes confusion, but with it division, destruction, and pain. The world that doesn't know God and today's public education system tells your child, "If you were born a girl but you feel like you are a boy, you can identify as a boy." Or worse yet, actively promote the idea to your child, to experiment with being the opposite gender. How evil is this in the sight of God? Adults are taking your innocent five and six-year-olds and planting seeds of doubt—what-if scenarios.

God made it clear; He created them male and female. Deuteronomy 22:5 says, "A woman shall not wear a man's garment, nor shall a man put on a woman's cloak, for whoever does these things is an abomination to the LORD your God." In other words, God is saying to accept who He made you to be—male or female—and not to alter, change, or transform from a man to a woman, or a woman to a man. If someone does such a thing, it is a very serious offense—it is an abomination (hated, detestable, and abhorred) to the Lord.

"He created them male and female in His likeness…to be fruitful and multiply." There won't be very much multiplication taking place in ten to fifteen years, if today's boys refuse to be boys, and girls claim to be boys and are attracted to other girls.

A pastor friend of ours said it well; "If the whole world turned gay today, what would happen to the human race?" Good question. The human race would be extinct. That's what the devil wants—to destroy God's creation and prevent God's command (to be fruitful and multiply) from unfolding.

Contrary to what the world believes, and even some churchgoers, homosexuality is a sin. It is a sin in the same category of sins listed in 1 Corinthians 6:9–10; "Or do you not know that the unrighteous will not inherit the kingdom of God? Do not be deceived: neither the sexually immoral, nor idolaters, nor adulterers, nor men who practice homosexuality, nor thieves, nor the greedy, nor drunkards, nor revilers, nor swindlers will inherit the kingdom of God."

I don't want to make light of this; however, some are quick to shout about how sinful homosexuality is (and it is), yet look the other way when it comes to thievery or greed—when all these sins are in the same *sin bucket*. If your work schedule dictates your church attendance, you may want to ask yourself if you are controlled by greed. I'm not talking about missing service here and there—life happens. Rather, I'm referring to a pattern of behavior. Do you find yourself choosing double pay over obedience to God and being in fellowship with your church family? Let's look at ourselves first, and show compassion for those around us bound in sin.

If you are struggling with homosexuality, feel like you are trapped, stuck in it, and don't know how to get out, there is hope. You can be delivered and healed in Jesus' name! There is deliverance from *all* sin in the name of Jesus! Confess your sin to a mature pastor that can handle your confession *and* pray for your deliverance. Homosexuality is a sin, but you do not have to be bound by it; you can be set free today, in Jesus' name, amen!

Dating

What is worldly dating? What is God's plan for dating and marriage? Let's discuss this important topic now.

One day, my ten-year-old son was playing an online game where you can play with other players from around the world. One boy he was playing with said one day, "I gotta go. My girlfriend is coming over." My sweet, innocent boy was taken back as we have taught him that you are friends with everyone (boys and girls) until you are bigger, and desire to get married. At that right time, we will pray and believe that God will send the right person for you, to you. We are not sure how old this boy was; but he was definitely a boy and clearly should not be having a girlfriend. This got me thinking and researching, and I found the following information.

Some adults said it's fine for kids to have a boyfriend or girlfriend as young as eight years old! What? One parent said that kids in school start dating in fifth grade, and others said eleven years old and fourteen years old is an appropriate dating age. Some said eighteen years old is a good age to date, and they we considered mean and irrational. Other parents said it depends on the maturity of the child. I have yet to meet some mature elementary, junior high, high school, or even a twenty-year-old mature and ready to date and commit to someone nowadays.

What does the Bible say about dating? Wise Solomon said, "Young women of Jerusalem, I charge you, do not stir up or awaken love until the appropriate time" (Song of Solomon 8:4). And further in verse 6, "For love is as strong as death, Jealousy as cruel as the grave; Its flames are flames of fire, A most vehement flame." In another passage, Solomon says there is a time for everything under the sun.

So what does all this mean? It means there is a time to be a kid, an adolescent, and later an adult. At each stage, enjoy where you are. Be patient to grow up. When you are mature and desire to marry, pray and ask the Lord to bring the right person into your life. If you dabble in dating prematurely, it will open up a can of worms, if you will, that you can't really close. You will desire sensual things (that are reserved for marriage) and have feelings for a girl or a boy that will drive you crazy. Your focus needs to be on enjoying childhood, sports, education, and friendships— and not on jealousy and fleshly desires. Premature dating leads to heartache, headache, and any other ache you can think of. Premature dating also leads to sin. If you experiment with "married couple things" outside of marriage, there are consequences, pain, and scars.

As King Solomon said, there is a season for everything. In godliness, enjoy the season you are in right now; and don't rush into the next season of life. At the appropriate time, when mature, desiring a husband or wife is a good thing; and God has many blessings reserved for married couples *only*. In fact, even *older* unmarried couples must abide by the same rules, obeying God's laws, remaining pure until marriage.

Parents, teach these precepts to your children, or just hand them this book to read, when you are finished.

Birth Control

While those *of this world* say children are a burden and expensive, the Word says, "Children are a blessing and a gift from the Lord" (Psalm 127:3). Furthermore, God blessed His people in Genesis—and told them to be fruitful and multiply! Birth control does just the opposite.

When I was young, the word *birth control* was still taboo, but today, people talk about it openly and use it openly. Birth control was introduced in 1960 by Margaret Sanger, the founder of planned parenthood. Most people don't know that the birth control pill does not prevent or stop conception (the moment when the sperm fertilizes the egg, thereby becoming a human life).

My Christian high school science teacher explained this well. The birth control pill causes turbulence in the uterus, making it difficult for the sperm to fertilize the egg. Should the sperm fertilize the egg, and should the fertilized egg survive the turbulence and implant in the uterine wall—during menstruation, the new life would be aborted. Certainly, we don't know how many pregnancies occurred in women over the years, then due to the birth control pill, ended in loss of life. Furthermore, adding these numbers to the countless amount of babies aborted through legal abortion (since 1973 in the USA) makes one grievously wonder how many needless deaths (in utero) have *actually* taken place.

According to Focus on the Family, they had the following to say about contraceptives; "Focus on the Family holds that all human life is sacred, and that life begins with fertilization (the union of sperm and egg). We don't believe that it's wrong to *prevent* fertilization, but we oppose any method of so-called birth control that functions as an abortifacient (any method that acts *after* fertilization to *end* a human life by preventing implantation in the womb)."

When my husband and I were dating, he said he wanted two boys and two girls. I didn't have a specific number in mind, however, I wasn't opposed to what his desire was, and was open to whatever God wanted for our family and future. Turns out, we had two boys and two girls, in that order. However, I still felt in my heart that God had at least one more child (a boy) to add to our family.

After some time, over a couple years to be more precise, my husband and I came into agreement—whatever God wants for our family, we are in. Shortly after this, maybe a few weeks, we got pregnant. I believe, based on God's Word, that whatever you desire and agree upon will happen; "Again I say to you, if two of you agree on earth about anything they ask, it will be done for them by my Father in heaven" (Matt. 18:19).Today, we also have a sweet baby *John*—a wonderful addition to our family.

The advice I want to share with my children when they are mature and wanting to get married, is the following: Talk to your future/potential husband or wife about what you want your family to look like—including children, schooling, career, travel, and what you desire to do for the Lord. Your agreement or disagreement on these topics will be a good guide to what your next steps should be—continue in the relationship toward marriage or part ways. There is power and peace when two people agree, and God will grant your hearts' desire.

Pressure to Perform

There is a huge focus on self today, and an enormous pressure to perform well, in this world's system. Children and adults feel this demand from the world around them.Furthermore, self-esteem is a big topic, and taught in American public schools. Certainly, there is healthy self-esteem—a sense of personal confidence required to engage in activities such as going to school, work, etc. without assistance. However, the world takes it a few steps further and says, "Believe in yourself, believe in your strengths, believe in your good looks, and believe in your wealth." This is the message—everything is based on self. Wow! That's a lot of pressure, especially when we fail. Surely, we all fail and have wins too, as both are a normal part of life.

The message of the Bible is very different; "Trust in the Lord with all your heart and lean not on your own understanding; in all your ways submit to him, and he will make your paths straight" (Proverbs 3:5–6). Furthermore, we see in Philippians 4:13 that our strength does not come from self, it comes from God Himself; "I can do all things through Christ who strengthens me." A Christian is *in Christ* and remains in Christ through obedience to His Word.

You can choose today to trust in yourself and your possessions, or to much more easily trust in God. When we choose to trust God, we are choosing that strong foundation; "The Lord is my rock, my fortress, and my savior; my God is my rock, in whom I find protection. He is my shield, the power that saves me, and my place of safety" (Psalm 18:2).

We all need a rock in our lives—something stable we can count on. When your rock or your foundation is Christ (and not your own abilities or the relationships that you possess), you win each time, and breathe easier. Even when you fail *in the eyes of the world*, you win—for in God's system, even the bad works for your good (Romans 8:28).

This Christian journey is a marathon, with ups and downs. However, alongside you *runs* God by His Holy Spirit; He will fill your path with great wonders—you can count on that!

Fear Not

When faced with stress, disease, or hardship, what do those *of this world* do? They panic. Unfortunately, God's people, those of His kingdom, at times panic and walk in fear also. Remember, we live in the world but are called by God not to be *of* this world or its ways!

Right now, in the U.S. and worldwide, we are faced with the coronavirus and talks of World War III. Conforming to the ways of the world is to panic. How should God's people be responding to this fear or any fear for that matter? After all, we have the Spirit of the living God on the inside.

Responding to this virus with a resolve to place all of your trust in God will provide peace in the middle of the storm. On the contrary, trusting anything else (man, media, or pseudoscience) will produce anxiety and fear; "Fear shows a lack of faith in God and His provision. But the Bible gives us many reasons why we can trust the Lord for His help" (www.whatchristianswanttoknow.com).

Philippians 4:6–7 says, "Be anxious for nothing, but in everything by prayer and supplication, with thanksgiving, let your requests be made known to God; and the peace of God, which surpasses all understanding, will guard your hearts and minds in Christ Jesus." I printed, framed, and quoted this scripture many times; and I placed it on the wall, near our front door, a couple of years ago. I've had my own struggle with fear, dating back to when I was in kindergarten. Quoting this scripture has delivered me from fear–many times.

The devil's plan and the ways of the world is for us to live in fear; fear has torment. God's plan is for us to have life, and life more abundantly. He desires for us to live by faith—placing all of our trust in Him, and placing all of our fears at His feet.

In addition to quoting scripture, another way you can arm yourself against fear is by thinking critically. It is crucial for Christians to judge everything they hear—whether it is heard from a pulpit, or a news media outlet, or a friend—check the facts. The early Church was encouraged by the apostles to go home and check the facts, and check the Bible. Why? To train the believers to not just accept anything they hear, but to make sure that what they are hearing is truth. In other words, the early church was taught to think critically; "Critical thinking is the intellectually disciplined process of actively and skillfully conceptualizing, applying, analyzing, synthesizing, and/or evaluating information gathered from, or generated by, observation, experience, reflection, reasoning, or communication, as a guide to belief and action" (criticalthinking.org). Today, critical thinking is a lost asset.

People, instead of being taught to think critically, have been taught to rely on the thoughts of others—*the professionals*. Public education, liberal media, and liberal government say, "You are not equipped to think for yourself; you are not knowledgeable enough to make good decisions; trust us (the professionals) to think and make decisions for you." However, what happens when the professionals lose their way—through human error, through false information (lies), or through corruption? Who will fact-check the fact-checkers?

Check the facts, and don't just accept what others say. Facts or truth will bring you peace, while lies will bring you anxiety and panic. If you are not sure what the truth in a situation is, wait. People feel uncomfortable with saying, "I don't know what the truth is." If you settle for a lie, thinking it is truth, there is no room for the real truth to be revealed, for you are no longer searching. Wait on God. He will give you discernment through the Holy Spirit, which is the Spirit of Truth.

Christians full of the Holy Spirit are God's physical representatives on this earth. We are the voice of truth, we are the calm in the storm, and we are the guide to a world that desperately needs Christ. We cannot afford to panic—for ourselves, for our families, and for the world around us.

Contextual Lies

From what I have been noticing and learning by mere observation, it has become popular and acceptable to tell part of the truth, while omitting some information. Or telling a truth, but setting it in a different context, and by doing so, change its original meaning. The media does this often— preachers do it too, intentionally or unintentionally. People in society, those *of this world*, tell lies so easily, so leisurely— destroying lives in the process.

Anytime we add or subtract from the truth, to change the outcome or meaning, this is deceit. Deception is the act of causing someone *to accept as true or valid* what is false or invalid. How often does this happen today? Too often. This behavior is almost expected of the world;however, God's children are called to a different standard, for *we are not of this world*. We must always represent truth.

The biggest form of deception is taking the Word of God and using it in a different context than it was meant to be used in. This can be done on purpose or through ignorance. Either one is dangerous—causing division, confusion, and fragmentation in the body of Christ. The Bible says there should only be a few teachers (James 3:1), a few that are full of the Spirit and knowledge of God.

Take the Word out of context is exactly what the devil did to Jesus. He used passage after passage, true words, but out of context, which makes them lies, to tempt Jesus. After Jesus was baptized, He was led by the Holy Spirit into the wilderness to be tempted by the devil. After fasting for forty days and forty nights, Jesus became hungry. This is when the devil comes to tempt, when Jesus is vulnerable. Surprised? Of course not, because the devil doesn't play fair.

In the same manner, the devil comes to tempt us when we are vulnerable. I've noticed that being hungry, tired, overworked, stressed, worried, lonely, depressed, financially unstable, sick in the body—anything that has to do with stress on the flesh—puts humans in a vulnerable state. Sin also puts us in a vulnerable, weakened state.

When Bible verses are taken out of context, you get different interpretations, disagreements in the church, church splits, and too-many-to-count Christian denominations. One source says there are 2.42 billion Christians—the largest religion in the world; there are nine major branches of Christianity, with forty-one thousand denominations. Who is at the base of this division? The devil.

Speaking of division, at some point in time,this seed was planted in the Christian community—to be careful about what *version* of the Bible is being read from, preached from, and studied from. This discussion has caused so much division, not unity. I looked at King James, New King James, English Standard Version,New Living Translation, and more in studying the various topics in this book. Studying one scripture in different versions did not derail my faith, but rather it gave me a deeper understanding and increased clarity of the subject, for all the different versions collaborated together.

The problem today is not that people aren't reading the *true version*, but rather that Christians are not reading the Bible—period. The Bible must be read, understood, and applied. If I struggle to read KJV because I don't speak "thee and thou language," I will not have a full understanding of what I'm reading *or* I will get so exhausted with trying to translate everything in my mind that I may stop reading the Bible altogether. Read the version that you comprehend—asking the Holy Spirit for understanding and help to live out what you've read.

The entire Bible is truth. It is crucial that each person understands the truth shared in the Bible, in the proper context. The Holy Spirit inside of us leads us in all truth. However, we must learn or train ourselves to recognize His voice.

The Bible is meant to be read daily. The more you read, the more likely that reading will transform into studying of God's Word, and obedience to what you've read. Then your soul will delight in the ways of the Lord! And you can live the truth for the glory of God and show others the way. When you lead others down the path of truth through teaching, preaching, and actions, you are considered great in the Kingdom of heaven (Matthew 5:19). Praise to the Father!

Sunday Is Coming

Lastly, in this chapter, let's talk about Sundays. We must also think differently about *Sunday.* How many of you are excited on Saturday, because tomorrow is Sunday? And not because you will be going to the ball park or watching the *big game.* David expresses in Psalm 122:1, "I was glad when they said to me, "Let us go into the house of the Lord.""

The fourth Commandment says to remember the Sabbath day and keep it holy. Unsurprisingly, the world has turned Sunday into anything *but holy.* Sunday is supposed to be a special day when God's children meet together; this can be reflected by wearing special attire. I believe you can honor God with wearing *a little something extra* on Sundays; something a little more special than what you would wear, let's say, to the park. I don't think you have to go over the top with a suit and tie *or* prom dress either. After all, in order to worship like David did, you need room to move around, and clothes that accommodate doing so—while also upholding modesty.

God presents Himself in His temple, among his beloved. Biblically, what should be happening in the church body and in church services are works and movement for the glory of God. *Living stones* are active, not inactive—they move around; and sad faces and stiff postures don't reflect the Holy Spirit— they reflect religion.

Movement and activities should be taking place for a very specific purpose—the perfecting of the saints and bringing glory to God. The Bible says in 1 Peter 2:4–5, "As you come to him, a living stone rejected by men but in the sight of God chosen and precious, you yourselves like living stones are being built up as a spiritual house, to be a holy priesthood, to offer spiritual sacrifices acceptable to God through Jesus Christ."

176

Outside of the four church walls, American Christian churches are known for doing outreach programs to bring in the unsaved, mission trips oversees to spread the gospel there, and programs to feed the hungry in the community. And inside of the four walls, they have used wisdom in how they conduct their services, making good use of the time on hand. My husband and I spent a good handful of years (at least ten years) in the American Christian community, and noticed the following:

- ❖ Members arrive early to church, use the restroom *before* service starts, and take their seat before service starts— as to not be a disturbance to others, and out of respect for the Holy Spirit who is present.

- ❖ Members take their children to children's church, where they will learn biblical principles that are true, fun, captivating, and on a child's level.

- ❖ There is a designated worship time—all instruments, voices, worship team, choir, and pastors worship together for a time of praise and worship. During this time, the altars are open, and people are welcome to come up and worship or to receive prayer.

- ❖ After worship, all worshipers (choir, band, worship team) take their seats in the sanctuary and an offering is taken—the tithe.

- ❖ Then the pastor, the person appointed by God to teach the flock, teaches the Word of God to the congregation.

- ❖ In closing, there is almost always an altar call, giving the unsaved an opportunity for salvation.
- ❖ Greetings, smiles, laughter, love, and fun are sprinkled in throughout the service.
- ❖ Counselors and pastors are available for prayer and counseling.

Love it! God is life and full of life, and we should be also. God is also purposeful in all He does, and we should be purposeful as well, using the time we are given wisely—whether in church or during the week in our personal time. In these areas, the American Christian church has been a great example for other Christian cultures to model.

I think it is worth talking about "what church service is not for." Church service is not for *entertaining* people through the preaching, worship, choir, band, or special music. Nor is it designed to pass the time or make you say, "Church was so nice today." It must be more than that. Church services should be like a battlefield—full-on warfare against the devil. Worship, preaching, and teaching through the Holy Spirit should be taking place—drawing people to repentance and magnifying the Lord.

Praises to God go up, and the walls of sin and shame come down, in Jesus' name! Ushering in God's presence is done by humbly submitting to the Lord, asking the Holy Spirit to move. Lights and smoke have nothing to do with it, so why bother? It's a distraction more than anything.

If I were a pastor, I would want to move as far away from the world's image and worldly ways as possible. Mixing the old—your former life without God and its worldly ways—with the new—a life full of the Holy Spirit—is not what God desires. We read in Mark 2:22, "And no one pours new wine into old wineskins. Otherwise, the wine will burst the skins, and both the wine and the wineskins will be ruined. No, they pour new wine into new wineskins." One online source says, "New wine needs a new wineskin because as the new wine expands during the fermentation process, it stretches the wineskin. An old wineskin will burst under the pressure of new wine." In other words, the ways of the world are not fitting, not compatible, with the ways of God.

We are commanded by God to live in this world, yet not belong to this world. The ways of the world are very different from the ways of God. We must have our thinking, our minds, renewed by the Word of God; the baptism of the Holy Spirit will help in this sanctification process. With a new mind, the mind of Christ, we will make great decisions—bringing glory to God and producing blessings in our lives and in the lives of those around us!

Chapter 7

The Ten Commandments

God showed His love for humanity by sending His only Son, Jesus, to be born as a beautiful, precious baby boy. Jesus grew up and lived as all other men and women. He was tempted in all ways; therefore, Jesus can relate to the trials you are facing. He faced the same trials and passed the test (never sinned). Because Jesus was and is an overcomer, we also are overcomers, if we abide in Him. Once we are saved, we ask and receive the same power, by the filling of the Holy Spirit who dwells in us, to overcome sin.

Jesus voluntarily (without any force from the Father, with love) gave His life on the cross for our sins; "There is no greater love than when one lays down his life for another" (John 15:13).God chose to love us, first, while we were yet sinners (Romans 5:8). How could you or I ever repay God for such tremendous love? We can't; however, we show God our love toward Him by obeying what He tells us to do. John 14:23–24 says, "Jesus answered him, "If anyone loves me, he will keep my word, and my Father will love him, and we will come to him and make our home with him. Whoever does not love me does not keep my words. And the word that you hear is not mine but the Father's who sent me.""

So God showed His love toward us by sending His Son to die on the cross—*we show our love toward God by obeying His commandments.* God wants obedience from His children. Why? I believe it is for the same reason I expect, and sometimes have to demand, obedience from my children. It is for their protection and for the purpose of shaping and molding them into the likeness and image of Christ. Notice that our obedience benefits us, not God necessarily. When we obey, great things happen in our lives as a direct result of obedience. Just like 1+1= 2, knowing God's commandments+ keeping God's commandments = blessings.

In response to all the *bad news* the media accentuates, some may say, "Why is God allowing all these bad things to happen?" or "How can a loving God do (fill in the blank)?" The truth is, *God didn't do it*. Mankind causes bad things to happen through their disobedience. Disobedience can be performed knowingly or disobedience can be carried out through ignorance. Either way, when we disobey knowingly or unknowingly, we are automatically heaping condemnation (chaos, confusion, destruction, evil) on ourselves. Any disobedience is an open door for the devil to enter. It doesn't have to be some major sin; it can be as simple as holding a grudge against someone for something they did years ago. Or overindulging (overeating), when the Bible teaches us to have self-control.

Now, let's look at Exodus 20; *The Ten Commandments* God left to Moses, and its practical application for us today. Let's know them. Let's obey them. Let's show God that we love Him (and also inherit blessings as a result)!

Commandment #1: "You shall have no other gods before Me."

Why would God tell us to have no other gods before Him? First, He is holy, He is the Creator of all things, and He deserves nothing but first place in our lives. Additionally, when we place other things before God, we prove to God that those things are more important, are our gods, our foundation. And when these gods fail us, we crumble.

God can be trusted to be a sure, solid foundation. When He is your rock, you will remain standing, even during trials. What constitutes as a god? I believe anything that takes priority over God becomes a god or *our god* in our life. Your job, your political party, or even your selfishness can be things that you rank above God. Your husband, your wife, or your children can be an idol if they take priority over God. Your position in the church, the *feel-good* sentiment of preaching a good message, or anything else that glorifies flesh—can be an idol. Any service we do in the name of the Lord must truly be for the Lord—zero percent of the glory belongs to man.

God must be first in every area of our lives. He is trying to spare us pain when He says, "Have no other Gods before me." Only then will we be stable, happy, fulfilled, and able to be used for every good work—when He is first in our lives.

Commandment #2: "You shall not make for yourself a carved image—any likeness of anything that is in heaven above, or that is in the earth beneath, or that is in the water under the earth; you shall not bow down to them nor serve them. For I, the Lord your God, am a jealous God, visiting the iniquity of the fathers upon the children to the third and fourth generations of those who hate Me, but showing mercy to thousands, to those who love Me and keep My commandments."

We don't hear much about people making statues today; however, statues exist in some Christian churches (Catholic, Orthodox). God's commandment says, do not make statues; do not bow to statues. God is a jealous God and will not share His glory with anyone. I think the main takeaway here is *worship of something other than God.* A statue, a picture, a tree for that matter, are all objects; however, it's what you do with them that matters. Do not worship anything but God almighty.

Commandment #3: "You shall not take the name of the Lord your God in vain, for the Lord will not hold him guiltless who takes His name in vain."

I believe anytime we don't use the Lord's name in the appropriate context, which is revering Him as holy, we are taking the Lord's name in vain. In the name of Jesus, there is power—power to heal, power to save. His name is holy and powerful and should never be used in a sentence to express our frustration, anger, or even surprise.

On the contrary, always use Jesus' or God's name to magnify who He is—He is holy. If you can control your tongue, you can control your entire body; "And if anyone does not stumble in what he says, he is a perfect man, able also to bridle his whole body" (James 3:2). Furthermore, regarding the tongue, James 3:9–10 says, "With it (our mouth) we bless our Lord and Father, and with it we curse people who are made in the likeness of God. From the same mouth come blessing and cursing. My brothers, these things ought not to be so." Lord, help us to revere your name as holy, and to bring our tongues under the submission of the Holy Spirit, amen!

Commandment #4: "Observe the Sabbath day, to keep it holy, as the Lord your God commanded you. Six days you shall labor and do all your work, but the seventh day is the Sabbath of the Lord your God. In it you shall do no work: you, nor your son, nor your daughter, nor your male servant, nor your female servant, nor your ox, nor your donkey, nor any of your cattle, nor your stranger who is within your gates, that your male servant and your female servant may rest as well as you. And remember that you were a slave in the land of Egypt, and the Lord your God brought you out from there by a mighty hand and by an outstretched arm; therefore the Lord your God commanded you to keep the Sabbath day."

First, how amazing that God commands us to take a break! We live busy lives, and if we don't stop to rest our mind and body, we put ourselves in a vulnerable state—a state that makes us weak. We are able to fight the battles of life more successfully from a position of strength; there are physical and spiritual battles to overcome. Remember, Satan came to Jesus when He was hungry or weak in the flesh.

The body of Christ (church members in particular) was designed for fellowship with God—and fellowship with one another. Meeting together as a church body on Sunday is essential to our Christian faith. The Bible says we are all parts of one body. We must spend time together, in order for God to use us to speak life to one another (admonish one another). Together, we rejoice in worshiping the Lord, in praying for the sick, in believing for miracles, and in agreeing on God's will with one heart and in one accord. If we are isolated at home, we are truly missing out. Notice the devil wants isolation, while God desires fellowship. As far as it depends on us, and we are physically able, we must strive to be present together physically—along with our minds and hearts.

After the resurrection and Jesus' ascension to be with the Father, there are Biblical examples of the believers being of one accord and united: "And when the day of Pentecost was fully come, they were all with one accord in one place" (Acts 2:1), and "They all met together and were constantly united in prayer, along with Mary the mother of Jesus, several other women, and the brothers of Jesus" (Acts 1:14). What does it mean to be of one accord? The Greek translation for one accord is "properly, with the same passion" and "having the same desire." There is power in being in one accord, being united.

If we love our brethren, when we are physically present together and we have the same passion and desire, for the Lord's will to be done—we are unstoppable for the kingdom of God!

Even though our salvation does not lie in church attendance, it is important for us to know this commandment, and obey this commandment, because no amount of money is worth us being absent from the gathering of the saints. And to keep a tab of attendance, personal or of others, is not the answer. Our heart should desire to be together with God's people. Hebrews 10:25 says, "And let us not neglect our meeting together, as some people do, but encourage one another, especially now that the day of his return is drawing near."

I think God is a big and awesome God and understands if you are new to a job and have no choice but to work shifts others with seniority refuse—like Sunday shifts. However, when the choice is ours, to work Sundays or not, what will you choose? God's house or double pay? Sadly, we fall in the trap. Unfortunately it happens more than one time, and we find ourselves habitually missing out on family time and fellowship time with our Christian brothers and sisters. But whenever we *obey* God's commands, blessings follow and never curses!

Commandment #5: "Honor your father and your mother, as the Lord your God has commanded you, that your days may be long, and that it may be well with you in the land which the Lord your God is giving you."

We can show honor to our parents with words, actions, respect, and obedience (childhood years). Never forget your parents, especially in their latter years. Take care of your parents' physical and emotional needs, when they can no longer care for themselves.

Commandment #6: "You shall not murder."

Murder is sin. Abortion is murder; therefore, abortion is sin. Most people will never hold someone at gunpoint and commit murder, thankfully. However, and sadly, abortions are committed by the millions. Globally, there are 125,000 abortions occurring each day. Abortion must be called what it is—murder. And abortions must be stopped immediately!

Because murder begins in the heart—anger, name-calling, and cursing must be dealt with. Two types of anger exist— righteous anger and unrighteous anger. Unrighteous anger seeks destruction, while righteous anger, which is godly anger and without sin, seeks restoration and rehabilitation. *Christians are allowed to be angry, but not sin* (Eph. 4:26).

To identify if anger is just (good) or unjust (evil), we must look at the heart of the matter. Is the heart motivated by God's righteousness (restoration) or by the flesh (our destructive and sinful human nature)? If the anger is motivated by the flesh, if we use words as a sword (to jab or destroy a person), this is unrighteous anger, and must be abolished. Lord help us!

There are times in the Bible when people or a person is called a fool, or a hypocrite. Is this considered name-calling and is this sin? No, it is not sin and here's why. As Christians, we must always be honest and speak truth; "...if calling someone a "fool" is simply objective truth, and *done not in anger,* but rather in rightly observing a person's state, then that is not sinful. So, it was not sinful for the Psalmist to say that people who say, "There is no God," are fools, because that is simply objective truth, and it was not sinful for Jesus to call the Pharisees "blind fools" because that was also simply objective truth" (reformedwiki.com). Christians must always *speak the truth in love,* not in anger, and always be motivated by righteousness. Lord help us!

Especially among Christians, we are never permitted to call each other fools *out of anger,* or to hold hatred in our hearts toward each other. We have been purchased with the same blood of Jesus, we belong to the family of God—therefore we must strive to love one another, forgive one another, and live in peace—united as one body of Christ (Matthew 5:21–22). The Holy Spirit calls us to repent of these things, asking the Lord and others that you have hurt with your words for forgiveness, and strive to live in peace.

There was a period of time, years after I got saved, when I would become so angry that I would swear. I knew it was sin, I didn't like it, but it kept popping up here and there in times of frustration and anger. I came to the Lord and I asked Him to remove it, and He did. After 1 or 2 weeks, the swearing was no longer an urge. I even stopped swearing silently, in my mind. Perhaps the key to deliverance was getting to the point of hating my sin, and not accepting it as a way of communication and expression—not justifying it. To *justify* means to show a sufficient lawful reason for an act done. I heard Lisa Bevere recently say that essentially what we justify, we can not be freed from. When we justify or defend ungodly behavior, we are coddling that behavior, holding on to it. Instead, we should be casting that behavior out, in Jesus' name.

Commandment #7: "You shall not commit adultery."

Be loyal to your husband or wife in thoughts, in actions, in public, and in private. One definition of loyalty says that "loyalty is the act of binding yourself intellectually or emotionally." The Bible says in Mark 10:8, "And the two are united into one" and continues in verse 9, "Therefore what God has joined together, let no one separate" or do not get divorced. Malachi 2:16 reads, "'For I hate divorce!' says the LORD, the God of Israel. 'To divorce your wife is to overwhelm her with cruelty,' says the LORD of Heaven's Armies. 'So guard your heart; do not be unfaithful to your wife.'" Certainly, this scripture applies to both husbands and wives.

Commandment #8: "You shall not steal."

Stealing objects, stealing votes, stealing ideas, stealing credit, or stealing of anything belonging to someone else—is all sin that needs to be repented of and never repeated.

Commandment #9: "You shall not bear false witness against your neighbor."

Always tell the truth about everything and everyone. One lie calls for another lie and so on. Whether you speak to one or one million people, the content must be true. The truth shall set you free (John 8:32), while lies will keep you in bondage.

Commandment #10: "You shall not covet your neighbor's wife; and you shall not desire your neighbor's house, his field, his male servant, his female servant, his ox, his donkey, or anything that is your neighbor's."

Be satisfied with what you have, and be happy for your neighbor. If it is difficult for you to do this, tell the Lord in prayer to help you, and He will.

"These words the Lord spoke to all your assembly, in the mountain from the midst of the fire, the cloud, and the thick darkness, with a loud voice; and He added no more. And He wrote them on two tablets of stone and gave them to me." How amazing! God spoke and wrote the Ten Commandments- then gave them to Moses, to share with God's people.

The choice is ours—to obey God's Word or not. However, there are risks or consequences that we will suffer as a result of disobedience. If we failed to obey any of God's Ten Commandments, we are not doomed; we have not lost our salvation; however, we must repent and ask God for forgiveness. God is a good God and desires for all to turn to Him and receive life and forgiveness.

In addition to the Ten Commandments, we find the great and first commandment, and the second, in Matthew 22:36–40; "Teacher, which is the great commandment in the Law?" And he said to him, "You shall love the Lord your God with all your heart and with all your soul and with all your mind. This is the great and first commandment. And a second is like it: You shall love your neighbor as yourself. On these two commandments depend all the Law and the Prophets." *Let's look at these two commandments in more detail.*

Love the Lord your God

God loved us first, and He commands us to love Him with all of our heart, soul, strength, and mind. He created you and everything else you see, and the things you don't see. He owns it all, including you, and He deserves all of our love and affection.

Why else does God tell us to love, to obey, and to serve Him only? If we don't purpose to love God and place Him first in our lives, by default we will love other things. The seat that should be filled by God will get filled by earthly things (love of self, love of money, love of career, love of the world and worldly things, misprioritized preoccupation with your spouse or children, lust of the eyes, lust of the flesh, risk of being a busybody, etc.).

We show God that we love Him when we obey His commandments (John 14:15). The *risk* of not loving God the way He expects is loss, frustration, emptiness, and sin in our lives. The *reward* for loving God is blessings here on earth and a paradise waiting for you on the other side of this short life.

Love your neighbor as yourself

God tells us to love our neighbor as ourselves. Why? God could have said, "Love yourself, love your family, and do what's best for yourselves." This not only sounds pretty selfish, but rings true of how humans act today and have acted selfishly throughout time. It is natural or human nature to be selfish—*it is godly* or a work of the Holy Spirit to be selfless.

How do we love ourselves? We take care of our body by feeding it, keeping it warm, grooming it, bathing it, spending money on it, and pampering it. This same level of care needs to be applied to our neighbor, those around us—starting with your spouse, then children, and all people we come in contact with.

The parable of the Good Samaritan describes well who your neighbor is (anyone you come in contact with) and how to treat them (with actions or works that prove love). If we are self-centered, bitter, and stingy, we cannot offer love to someone. In fact, you can't offer anything to anyone that you don't possess, including love.

We are God's representation on this earth. If we don't represent Him, who will? Ask God, by His Holy Spirit, to fill you—with the same love He has for you, a sinner. The love of the Father is sacrificial, loving in deeds, not just empty words. We can and must have this level of love—this perfect love—in our hearts.

Furthermore, this perfect love, this God-love—compels us to share the message of salvation with those around us. If you have family, friends, or co-workers that are not saved, and if you truly love them, tell them about salvation through Christ alone—speaking truth in love.

The risk of not loving your neighbor as yourself is strife, disagreements, chaos, internal emptiness, jealousy, and envy. If everyone obeyed this commandment—I loved my neighbor as myself, and my neighbor loved me as himself or herself—everyone's needs would be met, and there would be peace.

If my People

God commands us to love Him (through obedience to His Word), to love our neighbor (as ourselves), and to *humble ourselves and pray*. I believe the days of revival are right ahead of us, and the Lord God will cause righteousness and praise to spring forth before all the nations (Isaiah 61: 11). May all know truth, may all be saved, and may all be covered with the robe of righteousness and the garments of salvation (Isaiah 61: 10). *Christians*, in order for this to happen, in order for the Word to reach the entire globe—there is work to be done. The Bible says, "If my people, who are called by my name, will humble themselves and pray and seek my face and turn from their wicked ways, then I will hear from heaven, and I will forgive their sin and will heal their land" (2 Chronicles 7:14). This is what each Christian must do in order to see change—in order to be the living, active, powerful, relevant, life—giving body of Christ that this world desperately needs. Let's be obedient to God's

195

Word and see this nation and world be revolutionized for the glory of God the Father! How are we going to get it done? In four easy steps:

1. Humble ourselves. I become small so God can become big in my life. Recognize God for who He is—holy, all powerful, all knowing, and Creator of everything we can see and everything we can't see. Fasting will humble your flesh real quick. *Begin fasting and praying once a week if you are able.*

2. Pray. Pray when you are faced with fear, pray when you are faced with sin and temptation, and always pray to God as you would be talking to your best friend—sharing the good, the bad, and the ugly. Ask Him, not demand or command Him, to work His perfect will in your life. While you're at it, thank Him for all He has done for you!

3. Seek the face of God. How? Tell the Lord, "I want to know you and the power of your resurrection! Help me know you. Fill me and lead me by your Holy Spirit." Seek for God by reading His Word, the Bible, daily. God promises, "Seek and you shall find." Start with a one chapter per day commitment. Inspirational Bible verses on apps are helpful; however, in order to seek God and know God, you must read the good and the bad. If you only feed yourself with positive scriptures, you will be out of

balance. Just like you need to be reminded, "I will never leave you or forsake you," you also need to hear, "Repent, the kingdom of God is at hand."

4. Turn from your wicked ways. How? In our human nature, we are all wicked—Christian or not; "And I know that nothing good lives in me, that is, in my sinful nature. I want to do what is right, but I can't," says Apostle Paul in Romans 7:18. When you feed yourself with the Word and ask the Holy Spirit to baptize you, the Holy Spirit will fill you up, pushing out all the wickedness; and only in this way will you be able to obey God. In fact, it will be the Holy Spirit inside of us doing the good works.

Once we implement these four steps and make them our *lifestyle*, we can and should expect the fulfillment of God's promises—I will hear from heaven, I will forgive their sins, I will heal their land. Who wants to have their sins forgiven, and to see America and every nation healed? I do! I think you do, too.

Chapter 8

The Pattern of Sin

Have you ever thought about why and how the first sins were committed by mankind? Knowing the answers to these questions will give you a better understanding of this human flesh and God's solution for this sinful human flesh.

In Genesis 3, we find the *first sins* that were committed by mankind. The very first sin was disobedience. Eve, then Adam who was with her, ate from the forbidden tree. God allowed them to eat from any tree, except the tree of the knowledge of good and evil. God said once they ate from this tree, they would surely die. We know that they both ate. Both disobeyed and didn't die a physical death but rather a spiritual death. "Before they ate from the forbidden tree, they only had the knowledge of good—morally good, walking purely with God, innocent. After their sin of disobedience, they now had knowledge of evil, too—morally evil, separated from God, guilty" (cameronneace.blogspot.com). From this point, mankind was in need of a savior.

After the first sin was committed (disobedience), what happened next? Adam and Eve's eyes were opened, and they realized they were naked. Before sin, Genesis 2 says, "They were naked and unashamed," or it didn't even faze them that they were not clothed. What changed? It's possible that before sin, they were living in perfect harmony with God and did not need a cover. Now that sin was committed, they were no longer innocent and one with their Creator. Sin became the gap or distance between man and God. Now in order to be in the presence of a holy God, they needed a cover.

When they heard the Lord God walking through the garden, they hid. God asked of Adam, "'Where are you?' Adam answered, 'I heard you in the garden, and I was afraid because I was naked; so I hid'" (Genesis 3:10).

Likewise, when we sin, we hide. In fact, the devil encourages hiding and does not want us to come into the light. However, when we have sin in our hearts, it is so crucial not to hide, and instead, to come into the presence of God. When sin stays hidden, secret—it has power. But when sin is exposed, it loses its power.

Confession and prayer are biblical and have the power to break the chains of sin; therefore, "Confess your sins to each other, and pray for each other so that you may be healed. The prayer of a righteous person is powerful and effective" (James 5:16). Find a trustworthy pastor or a mature brother or sister in the faith to confess to, and they can pray with you, strengthen you, and keep you accountable. You may say, "Well, I confess my sin to God in prayer, in private." I think this is a good, biblical practice (1 John 1:9). However, sins that have us bound—those sins we continue to commit over and over—we cannot overcome them alone. Sin that remains in your heart and life is just like cancer to your spirit man. Obey God's Word, confess your sin to a Christian leader or friend, pray and be set free!

Next, we see in Genesis 3 that God asks Adam if he has eaten from the forbidden tree; and the response is not, "Yes Lord, I did, I disobeyed you." Instead, Adam blames Eve, and Eve blames the serpent. The pattern of sin is to hide from God and blame others for our sin. As long as we blame others for our wrongdoing, we will be stuck in the dark. We must look at the man in the mirror. When we pray, we stand in the presence of God, and we should spend time being quiet and analyzing ourselves. When we read God's Word, we also have the opportunity to analyze ourselves against the truth written in God's Word. That is why reading God's Word and prayer are both crucial to the Christian. We must come into the light so that our hearts can be exposed before God and cleansed.

After God explained the consequences Adam and Eve inherited because of their sin, God Himself made clothes of animal skin for them and clothed Adam and Eve. Interestingly enough, a head covering was not mentioned as being part of Eve's attire, as some Christians today believe that a head covering is necessary for Christian women. I suppose God could have made a head covering for Eve here, in Genesis, if He had so chosen.

Moving forward in the book of Genesis, it is written that Adam and Eve had their first offspring, *Cain and then Abel.* Cain worked the ground, and Abel had flocks of animals. One day, each son brought an offering to the Lord. Abel's offering was pleasing to the Lord—Cain's was not. The Bible doesn't give too much detail here, in Genesis chapter 4, of why Abel's offering was pleasing. However, scripture in the New Testament gives some clarity; "By faith, Abel offered to God a more excellent sacrifice than Cain, through which he obtained witness that he was righteous, God testifying of his gifts; and through it he being dead still speaks" (Hebrews 11:4). And in John, "[W]e should love one another, not as Cain who was of the wicked one and murdered his brother. And why did he murder him? Because his works were evil and his brother's righteous" (1 John 3:11–12).

If we look at *works* here or actions, the works of Abel were righteous; not only in how he offered sacrifices to the Lord, but in how he lived. Abel was a righteous man, and Cain was jealous of this. Why? Because of the evil in his heart. When Cain saw that the Lord was pleased with Abel's offering and not with his, Cain became very angry with God. But the Lord came to Cain and offered him a way out—a way of repentance; "Then the Lord said to Cain, 'Why are you angry? Why is your face downcast? If you do what is right, will you not be accepted? But if you do not do what is right, sin is crouching at your door; it desires to have you, but you must rule over it'" (Genesis 4:6–7).

God was giving Cain a do-over. If Cain would have made a commitment to do what is right, we can deduct that sin would not have been crouching at his door. He could have asked the Lord to forgive him for offering a mediocre sacrifice and made up for it by providing a new sacrifice that would be acceptable and pleasing to the Lord. *Likewise,* when we sin, the Lord draws our attention and calls us to repentance. However, God does not force us. We must yield to His lordship, ask for forgiveness, and repent. And then we can be cleansed.

Cain did not repent of his lousy sacrifice and anger toward God, and the sin sat in his heart and grew into jealousy toward Abel, which led to murder. He invited his brother, Abel, into the field and killed him. Then the Lord asks Cain, "Where is your brother?" Cain responds with arrogance and a lie; "I don't know. Am I my brother's keeper?"

What a tragic end to the relationship of the first brothers of mankind. How heart breaking this must have been for the Lord and for Adam and Eve. Unresolved sin grows into more sins, with bigger consequences. Sin begets more sin, and truly, the pattern is endless, unless you repent before the Lord.

How do we rule over sin? By doing what is right. Instead of trying not to sin, try doing what's right and just. And when we fail to do what is right, we come to the Father—asking for forgiveness—repenting by turning away from the sin, and being cleansed by the blood of Jesus. We all sin and need to be sensitive to the call of the Lord to repent *daily.*

God will never agree to or tolerate sin. However, there are specific things mentioned in the Bible that God hates. The Bible teaches *to love what God loves and hate what God hates;* "If we truly call ourselves Christians, we must not only love what God loves, but we must hate what He hates. This does not give us license to ever act hateful towards any individual; in fact we must love them deeper. It is the *kindness* of God that draws people into repentance. But we also cannot turn a blind eye towards the truths explicitly laid out for us in scripture" (jentezenfranklin.org). Therefore, it is important to identify what God hates and also hate what He hates, taking a stance in a dark world for the glory of God! Later in this chapter, we will also look at what God loves.

What does God hate?

1. God hates divorce.

Malachi 2:16 says (in two different translations):

> "For the man who does not love his wife but divorces her, says the LORD, the God of Israel, covers his garment with violence, says the LORD of hosts. So guard yourselves in your spirit, and do not be faithless."

> "For I hate divorce!" says the LORD, the God of Israel. "To divorce your wife is to overwhelm her with cruelty," says the LORD of Heaven's Armies. "So guard your heart; do not be unfaithful to your wife."

Notice God says he hates divorce. *God doesn't say he hates people who are divorced.* The heart of God is always to love, restore, and always to forgive. Why would God say that He hates divorce? I believe because divorce causes so much pain—for the couple and for the children. When husband and wife are joined in marriage and vow to be faithful to one another all the days of their lives, the Bible says, "The two become one flesh…what God has joined together, let no one separate" (Mark 10). When divorce happens, I believe it is like literally tearing apart violently that which has become one unit. To now separate what has become one is very graphic and malicious. The hurt, the pain, and the collateral damage is overwhelming. *That is why God hates divorce.*

Furthermore, marriage is an earthly representation of Jesus' commitment to His bride, His Church. This union is holy, binding; based on sacrificial, uncircumstantial, and unconditional eternal love. The world will see Christ in godly, Christian marriages and turn to Jesus as a result.

God is a God of peace, not pain. God does not wish for His creation to suffer. When a husband divorces his wife or a wife divorces her husband and then marries again, this is committing adultery, which is sin (Mark 10). Thankfully, God forgives our sin if we come to Him and ask for forgiveness.

A Christian Catholic woman, Patty Breen, who suffered divorce, explains divorce like only someone who has traveled the path can. Listen to the important things Patty has to say:

"I used to think people who got divorced saw it as an easy, quick exit ramp to something they wanted out of. Then it happened to me. I got married at 26—happy, naïve and very insecure. I thought I had the perfect Catholic fairy tale: Meet and date a former seminarian. Fall madly in love. Have a short engagement.

Get married, and start really living life because now I was fulfilled through marriage. Seven months after I got married, my world was utterly shattered. I learned that my husband was a sex addict and a compulsive liar. I was shocked. I felt numb. Everything I had ever hoped and dreamed for from the time I was a little girl was gone in an instant... I see a need in the church and am trying to listen to the voice of the Spirit to discern how I can help to fill this gaping hole in pastoral care. I want my church to speak up and speak out on the pain caused by sexual addiction. I want to hear priests preach from the pulpit on the evils of pornography. I want more than the occasional short letter from a bishop. I want the church to advocate for family causes beyond those related to pro-life issues and same-sex marriage. Catholic marriages are dying, and they need help and pastoral care. I am just one person. But the Spirit of God has lit a bright fire in my heart to be an advocate who challenges our church to speak to a reality that causes so much suffering in the lives of her members. I am still learning and praying about what that will look like in my own life and personal ministry. Our God cares passionately about the heartbreak and pain of divorce. For when God's children are in any kind of pain, it matters deeply to the heart of our Father. Yes, God hates divorce. But God never hates divorced people. In fact, God loves us, like he loves each person, with a love that endures all things" (America: the Jesuit Review, God hates divorce. But God doesn't hate divorced people).

I agree with Patty—the church must be relevant. We must recognize the times we live in, and the sins that are destroying youth, marriages, and families. God by His Holy Spirit can teach us all things—He can teach us how to help people battle sin and win.

If you are someone who is contemplating divorce, don't. Don't entertain the thought. God hates divorce. We should also hate divorce. Turn to the Lord with all your heart, and ask Him to repair what has been broken in your marriage. Pray to God and ask that your relationship with your husband, or wife, will be better than ever before. Find a Christian pastor to come alongside you. The devil and the world will always tell you the grass is greener on the other side. *Not true.* If this were true, God would have given the command, "If you feel like you are growing apart, just divorce the person you are married to, and your next relationship will be totally fulfilling." You will face similar challenges in your next marriage. Statistics show that after the first divorce, a second and a third divorce are more and more likely.

What is the answer? Turn your heart to God, both husband and wife. Read your Bible daily. Do what it says. Only God brings true wholeness to a person. Once you are whole, you have something substantial to offer in a marriage relationship.

If you are divorced but still single, pray for God's will to be done in your life. I believe God can still work miracles and restore marriages, even after divorce. If you are divorced and have remarried someone else, God is good and gracious and will work in our lives if we abide in Him.

I know some churches have marriage counselors, and all churches should. I believe trained Christian counselors filled with the Holy Spirit should counsel couples before marriage and also be available as a ministry to meet with couples and families as needed. I believe this need is great. People are facing marital and family issues, and they need a strong place of refuge to turn to—gaining victory for the glory of God! The church of Christ will only be as strong as its individual members and then families. When one member suffers, we all suffer. And looking the other way is very irresponsible and saddens the heart of God. We must take action!

Items 2 through 8 are sins God hates as described in Proverbs 6:16–19; "There are six things the Lord hates, seven that are detestable to him." I believe God specifically identifies these sins and hates these sins because not only does sin cause pain and destruction, but it also continues to spread and infect innumerous amounts of people. All sin must first be identified as sin, and then repented of, and restoration will follow in Jesus' name!

2. God hates haughty eyes.

"To have haughty eyes is to have an arrogant demeanor; it's an overall attitude of one's heart that causes one to scorn or 'look down on' others. The haughty person sets himself above others, and ultimately above God" (gotquestions.org). If you are reading this and fit this definition even remotely, may the Lord give you grace to see truth in your life and repent. It is important to note that God resists the proud. No one wants to put themselves in a position where he or she is resisted by the Creator of the universe.

3. God hates a lying tongue.

Lies separate us from God, lies destroy a country, and lies destroy trust between friends—for years to come. God hates a lying tongue. The truth is that we have each told at least one lie, right? "Who hit your sister?" "He did it!" they say, pointing to each other. We are born in sin; and if lying is not rooted out of our heart, it stays in our heart, damaging us and those we come in contact with.

People lie for different reasons. Some people tell lies to protect the image others have about them. Others lie to protect themselves from punishment. And some people lie on purpose with the intent of the heart to destroy someone because of hatred in their heart for that person. Women (or men) use emotions as a smokescreen, producing lies, and unfortunately, their lies are easily believed—when the facts should prove innocence or guilt in any situation. In fact, to establish guilt or innocence, two or three witnesses should be present—not one witness—who can easily be a lying witness (2 Corinthians 13). If you have suffered as a result of a lying tongue—do not fret! The Lord will reward you in due season (1 Peter 3:13–17).

Why else would someone lie? In the case of Ananias and Sapphira, they lied about their offering—pretending to give more than they actually did. In essence, they wanted the church to think more highly of them than they should. They could have said, "We sold some property for X, and we would like to donate a portion of that to the church." That would have totally been fine. But evil got in their heart. They wanted the credit of "giving it all." But they were actually reserving some for themselves.

When we get saved, this mentality of *reserving some for ourselves* doesn't fit scripture. To reserve a little sin here and there for ourselves—telling ourselves it's no big deal—will get us into trouble. We must give Jesus our entire heart. We must accept Him not only as Savior—but also as Lord.

If you have a problem with telling lies, ask God to forgive

you, and stop telling lies by starting to tell the truth. The Bible says to overcome evil with good—replace a bad habit with a good habit. It may be hard at first, but more than worth it once you conquer this sin. You will be a person people can trust, and this is admirable and godly!

4.   God hates hands that shed innocent blood.

God hates hands that murder, and we must also. We must do everything possible to protect life, specifically life in the womb. Abortion is murder, at all stages of pregnancy, for life starts at conception, regardless of how the pregnancy occurred —rape or non-rape.Let's face it, most abortions committed are non-rape, no abnormalities,perfectly healthy baby waiting to continue his or her life outside the womb, on planet earth. The doctors told my brother and his wife that their firstborn had Down Syndrome, and tried to convince them to abort. They are a Christian couple, and regardless of the health of the child, abortion was never an option—abortion was murder. Thankfully, my sister-in-law carried to full term, giving birth to a healthy beautiful baby with no abnormalities! The Christians in the USA and globally must take a strong stance against abortion and abolish abortion at all stages of pregnancy, in Jesus' name! Life must be protected in the womb. This is the Lord's will. God is the author of life, and we must protect life.

5.   God hates a heart that devises wicked schemes.

Imagine how sick or full of sin the heart must be if it is planning evil plans. This is not reacting off the cuff. This is carefully planning evil. There are people, and teams of people, that worship the devil, and work together to devise evil plans. They are strategic and their goal is to destroy God's plans. Lord, work even in the hearts of those who are devising wicked schemes, in Jesus' name. May they come to the knowledge and truth that Jesus is the Savior, and the answer to a heart that is infected with sin.

Furthermore, this truth, that oftentimes the wicked are more united than the righteous—should stir us up, should incentivise us—to unite as one body of Christ and accomplish great and marvelous works for the glory of God the Father!

Being strategic, being shrewd, is allowed for the Christian— while remaining obedient to God's laws always. Many times in the Bible, the term shrewd refers to the ungodly. However, in countless scriptures, shrewdness is tied to the wise. Lord, teach us today to be shrewd for your glory and for your kingdom!

6.   God hates feet that are quick to rush into evil.

A heart that is full of sin, and a life that hasn't received proper discipline, will be quick to rush to evil. We are born sinners. Humans must be trained in the ways of the Lord, and trained to follow law and order. Lord, have mercy on those whose feet are quick to rush into evil, and bring the disciple in their lives that will produce change.

7.   God hates a false witness who pours out lies.

A false witness not only hurts the person they are telling lies about, but it also hurts the person's spouse, children, family, friends, etc. There has never been such a time where truth is needed like today. People will tell lies for promotions, political gain, fame, fortune—you name it. We must get back to the truth and look for evidence, not just believing what someone says. Do everything in your power to be a true, credible witness. This is what pleases God.

8.   God hates a person who stirs up conflict in the community.

This behavior causes division, not to mention distress and chaos, and originates from a heart of unrest. God loves unity around truth. Problems can and should be resolved by uncovering lies and presenting truth, in a peaceful way. If you are a person who stirs up conflict in your community or church, today you can repent and ask God to change your heart and make you a man or woman of peace. You can be a pillar of peace, today!

These are the things that God hates—we must hate them too and cast them far from us, in Jesus' name. Instead, let's be known by our Godly character and characterized by *what God loves.*

What does God love?

❖ God loves eyes which gaze with humility

❖ God loves a tongue which speaks truth

❖ God loves hands which protect the innocent

❖ God loves a heart which devises good and righteous plans

❖ God loves feet which run rapidly to goodness

❖ God loves a trustworthy witness who speaks the truth

❖ God loves one who spreads peace among his brothers.

(crosswalk.com)

Sin in the heart is like putting on a blindfold, having blurry vision, or driving through a fog—your vision is severely compromised. How dangerous this is for you and for others! How can we fix this? Jesus says, "Repent!" "The **repentance** (metanoia) called for throughout the Bible is a summons to a personal, absolute and ultimate unconditional surrender to God as Sovereign. Though it includes sorrow and regret, it is more than that... In repenting, one makes a complete change of direction (180° turn) toward God" (wikipedia.org).

Sins must be identified as sins by pastors and preachers, then people can confess their sins, repent of their sins, and obey God's Word moving forward.

There is a saying, "When one door closes, another opens." In regard to our relationship with the Lord, we must purposefully shut the door to the devil. How? You shut the door to the devil by obeying God's Word. Submitting to the Lord's commands also opens the door wide open for Jesus to enter. He waits for us patiently, saying, "Here I am! I stand at the door and knock. If anyone hears my voice and opens the door, I will come in and eat with that person, and they with me" (Revelation 3:20).

God will forgive you of sin, and *you must also forgive yourself.* It is critical to move forward—forgetting those things that are behind; "Brothers and sisters, I do not consider myself yet to have taken hold of it. But one thing I do: Forgetting what is behind and straining toward what is ahead" (Philippians 3:13). In order to move forward, we must look forward. There is a time for reflecting, but that time should be only for a season. Then you must look forward and move forward.

If you find a pattern in your life of always looking back, always bringing up the past, ask God to help you figure out why this is. God will show you. Then you can settle it once and for all and move forward. When the devil brings up the past, rebuke him in Jesus' name! It will be hard at first, but then you will develop a habit of forgetting the past.

The devil wants you looking back, like Lot's wife did; she looked back and became a pillar of salt. Likewise, when we listen to the devil and constantly think of the past, instead of being the salt of the earth like Jesus commands, we become a pillar of salt—a statue that's good for nothing.

God tells us in Isaiah 43:18–19, "Remember not the former things, nor consider the things of old. Behold, I am doing a new thing; now it springs forth, do you not perceive it? I will make a way in the wilderness and rivers in the desert." In order to perceive what God is doing now—you must be living in *the now*—and not living in the past (nor living in the future). God wants to do new, exciting, life-changing things for us and through us—today!

Chapter 9

The Grace Umbrella

Once you are saved into the family of God, you enter a new covenant, a protection or covering called *grace*. Much like when a couple gets married, promises are made out of love, and a marriage license is issued—making it official.

Perhaps a certain amount of grace exists for all mankind— not just the saved. Certainly, Christians receive the gift of grace, by faith in Jesus; "But to each one of us grace has been given as Christ apportioned it" (Ephesians 4:7). From this scripture alone, it sounds like some people receive more grace, some less. However, each person receives as much grace as is needed, from Jesus Christ.

In our home, the *grace umbrella* is a multicolored enormous umbrella, and my kids and I would start off our homeschooling days praying underneath it. It served as a visual reminder that grace exists, and it was large enough to include all five of us.

It was each of our job to kneel in prayer, in silence, while each person prayed—agreeing in prayer, waiting your turn to pray. You could submit in obedience or get distracted, excited, and scamper off in disobedience. Then of course, some sort of punishment followed, as well as instruction to get back under the umbrella.

What exactly is grace? "Grace is the opposite of karma, which is all about getting what you deserve. Grace is getting what you don't deserve" (Christianity.com). Grace is the undeserved favor of God. Furthermore, grace works together with the Holy Spirit; "In the great proportion of passages in which the word grace is found in the New Testament, it signifies the unmerited operation of God in the heart of man, effected through the agency of the Holy Spirit" (Girdlestone 1871).

Entering under grace is a free gift and my good works or good behavior didn't place me under grace. We see this in Ephesians; "For by grace you have been saved through faith, and that not of yourselves; it is the gift of God, not of works, lest anyone should boast" (Ephesians 2:8–9). God created grace and gave grace to His children as a gift. However, it is up to me whether I remain under grace or not, right? This was my thinking for some time. If you obeyed God, you would be under the *grace umbrella*. But if you sinned and disobeyed, your actions would place you outside of the grace umbrella or outside of the grace of God.

However, this did not completely sit right in my heart, and I started to pray and ask God to show me what grace truly means. Grace is the *undeserved* love and favor of God. When do we *really* need grace? When we live in obedience to God or when we sin?

Apostle Paul writes in Romans 5:20, "Where sin abounds, grace abounds even more." By no way, shape, or form do we get kicked out of grace when we mess up—the grace umbrella just grows bigger! How awesome is God; His ways are above our ways. Man says, *three strikes and you're out.* God says, *a righteous man may fall seven times and rises again.* He's a good God!

In human thinking, when you and I obey we have essentially earned or deserve God's love and favor. But when we sin, we certainly do not deserve God's love and favor. What we deserve is punishment for breaking the law. Does this sound familiar? Breaking the law brings judgment, but Christ came to fulfill the law, paying the price for our sins, placing us in a new system that is opposite of the law, that system being grace. Praise God for grace!

If you are a parent, can you imagine your child doing something so terrible that you couldn't forgive him or love her any longer? As much as I desire for my children to walk in obedience their entire life (to God and to us as parents, while they are under

YOU WILL KNOW THE TRUTH

our authority), even when they make mistakes, the love aspect is never in question. Never. *Grace is love in action.*

"Where sin abounds,grace abounds even more" (Rom.5:20). Some may read this passage and say, "*Well this is a license to sin, right? The more I sin, the more God will forgive me.*" Not true. This passage shows how great God's love is for mankind. God understands that "the spirit is willing, but the flesh is weak" (Matthew 26:41). He also knows that in addition to battling the flesh, we also have to battle the devil. Once you are saved and you give your heart to the Lord, *the love of God constrains you* (2 Corinthians 5:14), or keeps you in a loving and faithful relationship with the Father. And the old life has passed away with all of its lusts and sin. Identically in marriage, the love you have for your husband or wife *constrains you* from seeking love or lust elsewhere.

Certainly, all sin separates us from God, however, don't use this truth as *a reason to sin.* Even when we do sin, God looks at the intent of the heart. Is the sin premeditated? Is it deliberate? Is it a force of habit? Is it a stronghold? A stronghold is something that holds you captive; it can be sin that holds you captive *or* thoughts that are not true, that hold you captive. Only God can break strongholds. We must be honest with ourselves before the Lord, dealing justly with ourselves, therefore we will not be judged like the world later.

If you call yourself a Christian and still sin constantly and feel no regret, you should question your salvation, to ensure you are not fooling yourself; "If anyone says, 'I know Him,' but does not keep His commandments, he is a liar, and the truth is not in him. But if anyone keeps His word, the love of God has been truly perfected in him. By this we know that we are in Him" (1 John 2:4–5).

Faith & fruit

If we are in Him, if we are born again (spiritual birth), then we have each been given a measure of faith—and our faith is evident through our works; "I will show you my faith by my works" (James 2:18). Faith defined is "the substance of things hoped for, the evidence of things unseen." Or you can think of faith as *hope in action.*

Faith is an action word. If I am believing and hoping for something, for example a prodigal son to come home, I am going to fast, pray, believe, and thank the Lord for bringing him back in Jesus' name! I don't just merely hope. My hoping is like an empty vessel. The vessel can hold something, and for Christians, that something has to be faith, not fear. Faith and hope coupled with actions or *works* will produce fruit. If my hoping isn't filled with faith and doesn't include actions or works, it dies and never produces fruit; "Faith without works is dead." Abraham provided the greatest example of faith in the Old Testament;"When Abram was tested by God in the matter of sacrificing Isaac, Abram obeyed" (Hebrews 11:17–19) and "showed to all the world that he is the father of faith" (Romans 4:16).

How can you and I have a living faith and produce an exceeding amount of fruit in our lives? Jesus says, "I am the vine; you are the branches. If you remain in me and I in you, you will bear much fruit; apart from me you can do nothing" (John 15:5). The vine has life, and as long as the branches remain in the vine, they also are alive. By themselves, unattached from the vine, the branches are dead. When the branches are connected to the vine, water and nutrition automatically flow from the vine to the branches—producing fruit. This *fruit* is the fruit of the Spirit, and includes the fruit of a life surrendered to the Holy Spirit—being the hands and feet of Jesus—doing those good works which he has planned for us to do ahead of time (Ephesians 2:10). We find the fruit of the Spirit in Galatians 5:22–23; "But the fruit of the Spirit is love, joy, peace, forbearance, kindness, goodness, faithfulness, gentleness and self-control. Against such things there is no law."

We remain in God through obedience to His word, and He remains in us when we open our entire heart to him each and every day, inviting His presence by the Holy Spirit to dwell in us. Then you will bear much fruit, doing the works *He* called you to do (not merely doing works that make us feel *good* inside).

Lastly, Jesus talks about the vine that doesn't produce fruit. He prunes it (some sort of discipline), gives it fertilizer (people full of the Holy Spirit to aid in your Christian walk), and time to produce fruit. He is patient. However, the day comes when He checks for fruit and the tree not producing fruit gets thrown into the fire. Why does the dry branch or tree get thrown in the fire? It was once alive and now is dead—useful to be used as firewood. This is not God's heart, but He can't force anyone to remain in Him. That is your job and mine. Abide in Him and He will abide in you; thus you will remain *alive* for Christ and produce an abundance of fruit your entire life.

Works vs. Gifts

I have noticed often enough in the Christian community the misuse of these themes—*works* and *gifts*. What the Bible says is a gift oftentimes gets misinterpreted as wages or something we have earned. A *gift* is not earned, or else it wouldn't be called a gift. A gift is something voluntarily transferred from one person to another without compensation; while payment or wages is receiving something, for doing something.

It   is crucial to understand what God gave us as gifts, so that we can have a full understanding of God's principles. Gifts from God are *salvation, faith, grace,* and *righteousness.* When you receive the gift of salvation, you also receive the gifts of grace and faith, as well as the gift of righteousness or right standing with God (Romans 5:17). Biblically, these gifts exist in our Christian lives simultaneously; you can't have salvation and righteousness, but be missing grace—it's all or nothing.

First, let's look at *the gift of grace*. The Bible says we have been saved by grace or unmerited favor, not works, so no man can boast (Titus 3:5). Some people live by a list of do's and don'ts, and judge others who aren't enrolled and engaged in strictly following *their* list. By doing so, essentially they are exhibiting their belief, through their actions, that salvation is through works, and not through grace. Such people are proving what God said would've happened if salvation was through works, that man would boast. Thankfully, we are saved by the gift of grace, and not by or through our own works.

Next, let's examine *the gift of faith.* In Galatians 2:16, Paul says, "Yet we know that a person is not justified by works of the law but through faith in Jesus Christ, so we also have believed in Christ Jesus, in order to be justified by faith in Christ and not by works of the law, because by works of the law no one will be justified." Even our best works or actions are tainted (Isaiah 64:6). Only faith in Jesus gives us entrance into heaven, and right standing with God, or *the gift of righteousness* (Romans 5:17). Both faith and righteousness are given to us freely by God himself.

Lastly, let's assess *the gift of salvation.* Nothing we can ever do in our human nature or human effort can be enough to earn God's salvation. On the contrary, *salvation is based on the works or actions God did.* God sent His only Son to earth to die an excruciating death, overcome death, and rise from the dead on the third day—to give us life. God showed His love for man through His actions or works. Thank you Lord for the free gift of salvation!

So where do *works* fit in the life of a Christian? When I think of *work*, I think of actions I am doing—giving an effort to accomplish a task. As Christians, our mission or greatest task is to reach others to join the family as well *(works)*. One of the ways Jesus used His hands and words to reach people, was through performing miracles (*works*). Jesus opened the eyes of the blind, raised people from the dead, cast out demons, and healed people of various illnesses.

Because of the miracles, people searched for Jesus and followed Him by the thousands. It's no wonder He would at times pray at night, the best time for Him to be alone with His

Father and have the least amount of distractions (Luke 6:12). God knows the human heart and the fact that people would be attracted to Him because of the miracles He performed. He knew that people were seeking for personal benefits; and what they would receive *are* personal benefits—both earthly and eternal benefits. Through the *works* that Jesus did, people received physical healing, and most importantly, they received salvation and eternal life! By the Holy Spirit, we can do the same miracles, the same *works*, drawing the lost into God's family.

Besides Jesus' works, there are many New Testament examples of *works*. Let's look into the actions or works of the Maltese people. When Paul landed on the island of Malta and spent a few months there, it says in Acts 28 that *the natives showed unusual kindness*, and later in the chapter, Paul healed all the sick on the island, through the power of the Holy Spirit. It appears that love (*works*) was a prerequisite to healings being manifest. Nowadays, a person gets healed here or there. However, God's plan is to heal *all who are present*.

At the end of this chapter in Acts, we find that the people of Malta further showed their love toward Paul and his team. They provided the necessary things for their departure—probably food for the journey was one of those things. The Maltese people showed their love through their actions.

In like manner, Christians should be generous and

hospitable, showing their love through their actions (works). You have heard that talk is cheap, and you can really see what is in someone's heart by their works or actions—not necessarily by what they say, unless their words are backed by actions (Matt. 7:16).

Rewards

When we walk in obedience to God and accomplish the work He tells us to do, are there rewards for these works? We talked about salvation being a gift, and to be in God's presence for eternity is more than a reward. However, what does God's Word teach about rewards for works?

Matthew 6 speaks of rewards; "Beware of practicing your righteousness before other people in order to be seen by them, for then you will have *no reward* from your Father who is in heaven. Thus, when you give to the needy, sound no trumpet before you, as the hypocrites do in the synagogues and in the streets, that they may be praised by others. Truly, I say to you, they have received their *reward*. But when you give to the needy, do not let your left hand know what your right hand is doing, so that your giving may be in secret. And your Father who sees in secret will *reward* you. And when you pray, you must not be like the hypocrites. For they love to stand and pray in the synagogues and at the street corners, that they may be seen by others. Truly, I say to you, they have received their *reward...*"

The Father has rewards for us and will reward us according to our works and the state of our heart, while we do those works —works such as having righteous deeds, giving to the needy, and praying for others. We see in 2 John 1 that one can receive a *full reward*. From this scripture, we can deduce that a person can also receive only a *partial reward* for their works on earth; "Watch yourselves, so that you do not lose what we have worked for, but that you may be *fully rewarded*. Anyone who runs ahead without remaining in the teaching of Christ does not have God. Whoever remains in His teaching has both the Father and the Son..." *When we remain obedient to God in all things: family life, church life, job life, and personal life—we will receive a full reward.*

To put a red bow on this chapter, grace is the undeserved favor of God, and can not be earned. Grace is a free gift. Salvation is a free gift—however the baggage (sin) must be left behind. Until your last breath, God's grace reaches out. Wisdom says, don't wait until your dying breath to repent! There is a big and beautiful plan that God has set apart *just for you*—to show you His love, to provide purpose and meaning to your life, and to give you life in abundance!

Chapter 10

God Is a God of Order

In everything that exists in the heavens, and on the earth, there is perfect order established by God. When godly order is respected and followed, all things seen and unseen run smoothly. God has established *law and order* in society, in the church, and in the family. To ensure peace and tranquility, law and order must be honored and obeyed. God is a God of order—not chaos, confusion, and lawlessness.

Order in Society

The Bible says in the last days lawlessness would abound; "And because lawlessness will abound, the love of many will grow cold" (Matthew 24: 12). What will characterize people in the last days? Lawlessness. Lovelessness. We read in Timothy, "But know this, that in the last days perilous times will come: For men will be lovers of themselves, lovers of money, boasters, proud, blasphemers, disobedient to parents, unthankful, unholy, unloving, unforgiving, slanderers, without self-control, brutal, despisers of good, traitors, headstrong, haughty, lovers of pleasure rather than lovers of God, having a form of godliness but denying its power. And from such people turn away!" (2 Timothy 3: 1–5). We know that the people of God must be different—full of the Spirit, abounding in the fruit of the Spirit, abounding in law and order.

Can you think of someone in recent history who stood for law and order? How about in early American history—like our founding fathers? Many of them were Christians, and also active members in their church. It is no wonder that their thinking, their mindset, was as follows; "We the People of the United States, in order to form a more perfect Union, establish Justice, insure domestic Tranquility, provide for the common defense, promote the general Welfare, and secure the Blessings of liberty to ourselves and our Posterity, do ordain and establish this Constitution for the United States of America" (Preamble to the U.S. Constitution).

These words in our constitution line up with scripture; for the Bible stands for life, liberty, freedom, defense of truth, and all things pertaining to truth and justice. Unfortunately, some groups in this country are trying everything possible to nullify this constitution. We must not allow this to happen for ourselves, for our children, and for our grandchildren (should the Lord tarry).

Moving forward, what does the Bible say about following the laws of the land? The Bible tells us to submit to government, to submit to the laws of the land; "Let everyone be subject to the governing authorities, for there is no authority except that which God has established. The authorities that exist have been established by God" (Romans 13:1). Additionally, 1 Peter 2:13–17 says, "Submit yourselves for the Lord's sake to every human institution, whether to a king as the one in authority, or to governors as sent by him for the punishment of evildoers and the praise of those who do right. For such is the will of God that by doing right you may silence the ignorance of foolish men. [Act] as free men, and do not use your freedom as a covering for evil, but [use it] as bond slaves of God. Honor all men; love the brotherhood, fear God, honor the king."

When we obey the laws, lives are preserved, and peace is maintained—laws such as obey the speed limit, wear your seatbelt, don't text and drive, and don't drink and drive, for example. The risk or consequences of not obeying the laws of the land are fines, loss of privileges, imprisonment, and even lives lost.

Any laws created that do not line up with The Constitution, that contradict the Word of God, that are not based on facts and truth—must be abolished. As Christians, God does not require our adherence to laws that violate His Word.

When the laws of the land violate God's laws of life, freedom, truth, and justice—we abort the law of the land and follow the Holy Spirit's leading. This is what happened to Daniel's friends in the Bible; "There are some Jews whom you put in charge of the province of Babylon—Shadrach, Meshach, and Abednego—who are disobeying Your Majesty's orders. They do not bow down to statues and worship other Gods." These three men refused the king's orders because the king's orders violated God's commandment to not worship any other gods and to not bow down to statues. Likewise, today we don't have statues around much; however, we must not bow down to anything that is *false*. We have the responsibility to have the mind of Christ—the mind of truth. We must seek truth until we find it. Once we find it, we hold tight to it, standing fast, and also share truth with others. We are exhibiting love for our neighbor, the second greatest commandment, when we share truth with our neighbor.

Law and order is important in society. But even more importantly, society or mankind needs *prayer*. God's heart is for all to be saved, and His Word tells us to pray for all people—including and specifically for world leaders and their salvation. We read in 1 Timothy 2:1–4, "First of all, then, I urge that supplications, prayers, intercessions, and thanksgivings be made for all people, for kings and all who are in high positions, that we may lead a peaceful and quiet life, godly and dignified in every way. This is good, and it is pleasing in the sight of God our Savior, who desires all people to be saved and to come to the knowledge of the truth." If Christians don't pray for world leaders, who will? We must pray for all world leaders, for all people—that God would reveal truth and save. And When world leaders get saved, they can impact their country and world for the glory of God!

Lastly, as we live in society, God tells us to respect order in the workplace, submit to the boss, and to work for our employer as if we are working for God. We see this in Colossians 3:22–24; "Bondservants, obey in everything those who are your earthly masters, not by way of eye-service, as people-pleasers, but with sincerity of heart, fearing the Lord. Whatever you do, work heartily, as for the Lord and not for men, knowing that from the Lord you will receive the inheritance as your reward. You are serving the Lord Christ." If you have a great boss, a mean boss, a lazy boss, or a controlling boss—whatever the case, while they are your employer, God calls you to submit to their authority (as long as their directions do not violate God's Word). When we do so, we are actually submitting to the Lord, obeying Him, and bringing glory to His name. A pastor friend of ours often said that Christians should be the best employees. I agree. God's people should be the best performers, the most submissive, and most respectful employees. Submission in the workplace is another way the world will know that God exists and that God is good.

I worked a sales job in pharmaceuticals for eight years. I worked very hard, to say the least, as if it were my own company. My last full year with the company, I earned *second* in sales in my state. The following spring/summer, I was laid off, while many others were not. Ultimately, I was just an insignificant employee, and all of my hard work meant nothing... BUT GOD! In God's kingdom, all of my hard work will be rewarded, in the time of God's choosing. He is faithful and does not remain indebted to anyone. Payday is coming. If you have a similar story, continue to work faithfully wherever you are, and God will be the one to promote you, even if promotion means leaving one job to take on an entire different career path.

Order in the Church

I am finding that the principle of submission is so crucial. If we can learn to submit to man, we will more likely submit to the Lord. A huge part of the Christian life pertains to submission, as does the Muslim religion. The big difference is that our submission is based on truth: Jesus is the Son of God, Jesus came in the flesh, Jesus paid the price for my sin on the cross with His life, and Jesus resurrected on the third day and lives forevermore!

Synonyms for submission are compliance, conformity, subordination, and obedience (Merriam Webster). The *opposite* of submission is defiance, disobedience, self-will, and rebellion. *Keep in mind*, biblically submission is submission to truth, and never complying just to comply. If you are ever asked to comply to anything based on falsehood, stand-up against it, do not conform, do not comply, for this is our Christian duty to stand for truth and not bow to anything false.

In the church body you belong to, it is God's command that each person submit to the pastor, submit to the church leadership, and submit one to another. First, let's look at submission to the pastor and leadership; "Obey your leaders and submit to them, for they keep watch over your souls as those who will give an account. Let them do this with joy and not with grief, for this would be unprofitable for you" (Hebrews 13:17). If you find you cannot follow this command, ask the Lord to help you get rid of this defiance. In order for God's presence to move freely and fully in His church, submission to authority must be present. Whether you think the pastor is doing a good job or not, it is the church body's duty to pray for the pastor, the leadership, and their families. The Lord will hold the pastor and leadership accountable for the work that they do. We must not burden ourselves with their performance. Let's be concerned about our own obedience and pray for one another—for the Lord's will to be done. God works through love, unity, and submission to His Word.

Let's not forget the other portion of this scripture in Hebrews 13; "Let them do this with joy!" Too many pastors are beaten up—instead of being lifted up—in prayer. Do you see areas in the church body that could improve? Surely you should be able to have a discussion with your church leadership regarding your grievances, at the proper time (a scheduled appointment) and with the right heart and attitude (truth spoken in love). But even more importantly, fast and pray to see God's will done in your church. Fasting and praying will produce results and changes, led by the Holy Spirit.

Lastly, God teaches Christians to submit to one another, to see your brother as better than yourself, and to love your neighbor as yourself. When this is done, there is mutual respect and understanding in a church body, where God can work as He wills. The results of *not* submitting one to another are strife, anger, bitterness, and unrest. This rebellious behavior is not characteristic of a sheep (but rather a goat or a bull). Like sheep, let's submit to church leadership, let's submit one to another, for this is God's will.

Order in the Family

In the family, like the church, the order established by God is perfect. Each person has their own role or calling, that

236

they are most suitable for. The order God established pertaining to the family is God first, then Jesus, next husband, then wife (1 Corinthians 11:3). The Husband and wife are *equal in value*, despite having different roles.

The chain of command flows from God to Jesus. John 5:19 says, "Jesus gave them this answer: 'Very truly I tell you, the Son can do nothing by himself; he can do only what he sees his Father doing, because whatever the Father does the Son also does.'" Jesus didn't have his own way of doing things. He submitted himself to the Father in all things and only spoke of and did what He saw the Father doing. When Jesus walked this earth, he was the perfect living example of how we should live, also, as children of God. *Through actions*—Jesus showed us God the Father.

After Jesus, the next in the hierarchy is the husband. God wired the husband to lead and receive from Jesus what direction the family should take. Please note that biblically men and women are equal, and can lead *in society*. However, in this section, we are looking at order specific to *marriage*.

So the husband's directions are found in God's Word, the Bible, the same place Jesus received directions for His life from God the Father. The Word, in conjunction with the Holy Spirit, serves as an internal compass. A husband must be spending time with God in order to hear from God. Husbands must crucify their flesh and humble themselves daily. Being perfected into the likeness and image of Christ is a life-long process. It will be easy for a wife to submit to a replica of Jesus, right? However, regardless of where the husband is on his journey with the Lord, the Bible commands the wife to respect her husband and be submissive to him (Ephesians 5:24, 33). Certainly, God would never ask a wife to take physical or verbal abuse from her husband—instead, she should run to safety and seek help and guidance from a pastor.

Seemingly, husbands have a lot of power and could easily abuse their power. Yes, this is possible. However, the husband is accountable to Jesus for all of his actions and the Word of God sets guidelines for husbands as well. First, the husband's prayers will not be answered if he treats his wife harshly (Ephesians 5, Colossians 3). Additionally, Ephesians 5:33 says, "However, each one of you also must love his wife as he loves himself." In the same chapter, husbands are commanded to love their wives *like Christ loved the church*; He gave His life for her. Giving your life for someone *means* putting their needs before your needs. Probably the greatest gift you can give your wife daily is to ask, as often as possible, "What can I help you with?" This very phrase will be a launching pad into a sweeter relationship—guaranteed. Certainly this goes both ways—wives toward husbands, too.

Why would God give this command to husbands anyways, to *love their wives like Christ loved the church?* I believe God's desire is to have an earthy symbol that people can see and relate to; marriage between a man and a woman symbolizes the relationship Jesus has with His bride, the church. Jesus loved us so much that he not only was *willing* to give His life, but He did in fact willingly *give His life for us.* In return, the church's responsibility is to submit to the authority of Christ. Who has the harder job? Jesus and husbands *or* the church body and wives?

Furthermore, this command *to love your wives like Christ loved the church* was given to husbands because this type of love is what makes a wife flourish. When someone is truly loved, it is like a flower that goes from being a bud to being in full-bloom. She has reached her maximum beauty, maximum potential, and is unstoppable for her family and for the kingdom of God! If she lacks this kind of love, tragically, it will result in her feeling insecure, unhappy, and emotionally unbalanced.

What makes a husband flourish? What I've noticed is that when a husband is shown *respect*, when he is considered worthy of high regard, he is able to operate at maximum strength and be the leader God created him to be. On the flip side, if a man feels disrespected, he will be provoked to anger. When the wife *submits* to her husband as the head of the family, it allows him to receive from *his head*, Jesus, all that is necessary for the family. It's not that God can't or will not communicate to the wife; He does. However, the husband's main role is to be the leader. It's funny, but not really funny, how women want a big strong man; yet, once they marry the big strong man, *some* women suck the life out of their husbands, and turn him into a weak man—through being unsubmissive and disrespectful toward their husbands.

Is submission for wives only? No. We read in Ephesians 5:21, "Submit one to another," meaning husbands or anyone in authority is not given permission to rule like a dictator. It also means *consulting with one another* always brings the best solution in any situation. A husband-and-wife work best, and the best outcomes are produced, when they work together. There are great qualities that both a wife and husband possess; tapping into those great qualities is wise, and two heads are better than one. One renowned pastor, Jimmy Evans, said he does not make a decision unless he and his wife are in agreement. Instead, they wait. Waiting and praying for God's will trumps forcing a decision, just because you (husband) are the head. Nonetheless, the man must be allowed by his wife to be the man, the head, in order for God to flow properly in the family. So far, I haven't seen anyone walking around with two heads—*have you?*

You may be a wife that has done her part (submit to and respect her husband), but your husband has not reciprocated with loving you like Christ loved the church, giving His life for you, putting your needs before his. Or you may be a husband who *has* loved his wife like Christ loved the church, however your wife *still* is unsubmissive and treats you with disrespect. If you fit either category, husband or wife, *pray* and ask God to work daily in your marriage—and He will!

We must each know our part, do our part, regardless of whether or not your spouse is doing their part. You do your part, or obey God's order, *because you love the Lord.* In order for biblical promises to be fulfilled in our families, God's order must be followed, and then the blessings will flow automatically as a result. This order in the family and the importance of the roles of husband and wife are so critical that Apostle Paul had to set down some rules, that we must heed to.

If you are a wife who struggles with submission, don't worry, I was there too. I had expectations for my husband and tried daily to make him fit *my mold.* I was trying to control him and everything else in my life. One day, God showed me that I had control over nothing. It broke me, but in a good way (Matthew 21:44). I was living my Christian life the best way I knew how; but God, in His love and mercy, saved me from myself. I completely took my hands off the wheel and allowed God to shape and mold me, mold my husband, and mold my children—into His likeness and image. What an insult it was to God when I was trying in my own power to do the shaping and molding. With my actions, I was telling God, "I do not trust you." And I asked myself if I knew God very well at all. Perhaps I knew Him, but didn't know how to trust Him.

I'd been a Christian most of my life, yet I just came to realize that my relationship with Jesus was superficial. In order to know Christ and the power of His resurrection, you must dig deeper. In order to get to the deeper things in God, you must obey His word, His entire word. *There is no other way.*

Disobedience to the laws of marriage set by God is not without consequences, and any disobedience to God's Word is a door for the devil to enter and cause chaos. If your marriage is struggling, your children will feel it too; while a strong, godly marriage produces confidence and stability in your children. The sooner both husband and wife obeys God's order for the family—the better. *Choose obedience*—for your marriage, for your children, for your family, and for the kingdom of God and His will. The world will know God by the love and unity demonstrated in Christian marriages.

Last but not least, there is a role for *children* in the family. Children are to obey their parents and honor their parents. Ephesians 6:2–3 says, "Honor your father and mother" (this is the first commandment with a promise), "that it may go well with you and that you may live long in the land." Children must be disciplined and *discipled*—the process of making someone become like Christ. If you "let kids be kids," the disobedience in their heart that they are born with will grow bigger and bigger. Parents are to discipline their children but also not push them to wrath (Ephesians 6:4).

When we had our firstborn, Ezra, I knew little about disciplining children—despite reading books on child psychology and raising children. What do you do with a one-year-old or two-year-old who refuses to stand in the corner...? They simply walk away.

It took years of parenting stress before I cried out to God for help. Uncoincidentally, I then ran across this great godly book on Amazon one day: *14 Gospel Principles of Parenting* by Paul David Tripp. It talks about the heart of the child.

This book was a great step in the right direction for our family. It helped me understand my children and humans in general. We are born in sin. We are born rebellious. The rebellion must be rooted out in Jesus' name! And just because you are an adult today does not mean you have learned obedience. Obedience is an issue of the heart. In God's school, you can't move up in the things of the kingdom, if you don't learn obedience to God's Word.

After encountering this helpful book, we discovered another godly parenting book. God led my husband to speak to a Christian man in Arkansas on my dad's farm. He has seven children who are very well-mannered and helpful. My husband asked, "How do you do it? We are losing our marbles!" The Christian brother recommended the book *To Train Up a Child* by Michael and Debi Pearl—which talks about training and discipline (among other topics). Proverbs 22:6 says, "Train up a child in the way he should go, and when he is old he will not depart from it."

Furthermore, Proverbs 22:15 says that "Folly is bound up in the heart of a child, but the rod of discipline drives it far from him." And, "Whoever spares the rod hates their children, but the one who loves their children is careful to discipline them" (Proverbs 13:24). *We were missing the rod in our parenting.* All we wanted was peace in our home. Proverbs 29:17 says, "Discipline your son, and he will give you rest; he will give delight to your heart."

The risk of not disciplining your child is chaos in your home and long-term negative effects for your child, putting salvation in jeopardy. If we as parents can't manage to discipline our children and teach them to submit to authority while we have authority over them, they will have to learn submission in the world. In the world, rebellion has consequences—consequences such as jail time, drug

244

addictions, bad relationships, car accidents with potentially grave consequences, etc.

Parenting can be rewarding for the child and the parent, once parents also address their own issues—issues of control, issues of anger, and issues of rejection. Once God touches our issues and makes us whole, we can effectively parent each child based on their individual God-given qualities, needs, and strengths—not our own hopes, fears, and dreams for our child.

In this busy life—with two working parents, school, sports practices, ballet, music lessons, and the list goes on—it is easy to get caught up in the whirlwind of crazy and nonproductive schedules. It is also easy to find that days, weeks, and years have passed—and our kids are *grown*. Time spent with our children—before they become adults—is valuable.

I believe in order to follow biblical principles, at least one of the two parents must actually be present. Deuteronomy 6:7 talks of parents teaching their children God's laws; "You shall teach them diligently to your children, and shall talk of them when you sit in your house, and when you walk by the way, and when you lie down, and when you rise." In order to obey this portrait of parenting, you must be present.

Parenting is shaping and molding our children into the likeness and image of God, and that is a full-time job. In order to do the job, you as the parent must be present, your children must be present, and godly principles must be understood and applied. In our home, we are blessed to homeschool our kids. It is easy to obey this scripture from Deuteronomy when you educate your own children. Ordinary, daily moments and daily interactions can be teaching moments—if you are vigilant—looking for opportunities to prepare your child for a successful future, and more importantly prepare them for eternity. Whoever plants the most seeds first, wins. Kids are quick to absorb information. Take advantage of this truth, and plant the Word of God, plant superior education, plant love and compassion, and plant friendship—that will last a lifetime.

God's order for the family is perfect, and blessings manifest when we obey His commands. Remember—husband, wife, and children are equal in value, equal in the sight of God, despite having different roles. God also has established order in the church, and in society. When order is respected and followed, we can expect wonderful outcomes in our families, in our churches, in the workplace, in government, everywhere—for obedience always produces blessings!

Chapter 11

Malachi

The book of Malachi is four chapters of *marvelous insight* and practical application. It is a quick read, yet full of many pearls. Read it slowly, or read it twice, to ensure you don't miss out on any good information. It runs parallel to the days we are living today.

Malachi is the last book of the Old Testament, and the book just before the four gospels in the New Testament. It is significant in that God spoke here, to Malachi, and didn't speak again through a prophet until John the Baptist, 400 years later. God was silent for 400 years.

Certainly, God was still present, and has been speaking through creation since the beginning of time; "The heavens declare the glory of God; the skies proclaim the work of his hands. Day after day they pour forth speech; night after night they display knowledge. There is no speech or language where their voice is not heard" (Psalm 19).

So who wrote this wonderful book? "The author is unknown; *Malachi* is merely a transliteration of a Hebrew word meaning "my messenger"" (britannica.com). Some say it may have been the scribe Ezra. Whoever the prophet was, God spoke, and the prophet listened, and then shared God's Word with the Israelites. These same words transcend time, and speak clearly to us today. You will see what I mean as we begin to study each chapter together.

Chapter 1

God's first message, the first sentence, is for *all Israelites*, and says, "I have loved you deeply." God loves Israel (and all humanity); however, in return the Israelites offered polluted offerings. They brought the lame, the sick— instead of offering their best or offering *a pure offering*.

God commands the Israelites to offer pure offerings moving forward, and to offer incense. What is the significance of incense? "As with most aspects of Old Testament worship, incense was a symbol that pointed to a greater reality. The aroma of incense was a physical picture of the prayers of God's people wafting up to heaven: Let my prayer be accepted as sweet-smelling incense in your presence" (jesusway4you.com). God is telling His people to *return back to prayer*.

God concludes this chapter with saying, "For I am a great King… And My name is to be feared among the nations" (Malachi 1:14). To fear God is to revere Him as holy, and to serve Him only, as the one true God. Furthermore, we see in Proverbs 1:7, "The fear of the Lord is the beginning of wisdom, but fools despise wisdom and instruction." *The fear of the Lord* must come back to the church.

Chapter 2

God's message starts with a word for *the priests*: "Listen, you priests; this command is for you!" He addresses leaders and priests and tells them to take to heart, to give glory to God's name, to offer incense and pure offerings. God tells the priests to follow Levi's example; Levi feared God, was reverent before God, the law of truth was in his mouth, injustice was not found on his lips, he walked with God in peace and *equity* (the quality of being fair and impartial), and he turned many from iniquity.

Malachi 2:7 says, "For the lips of the priests should keep knowledge, and people should seek the law from his mouth; for he is the messenger of the Lord of hosts." Who is the messenger of the Lord? The priest or pastor—ordained of God to teach the Word to its congregation.

Instead of being like Levi, being just, the priests have departed from the way, caused many to stumble at the law, corrupted the covenant of Levi, and have shown partiality in the law. Because of their actions, God sends a curse over their blessings.

In verses 10–16, God gives instructions to men and tells married men, *do not deal treacherously with the wife of your youth.* Treacherous means faithless, false, disloyal, untrue to what should command one's fidelity, betrayal, and disrespect. The *opposite* of treacherous is candid, equitable, fair, faithful, frank, genuine, good, honest, true, trustworthy, and upright. These are the qualities that should characterize married men and married women—a map showing how to treat each other daily. Be faithful, be good, and allow your spouse to be honest with you—instead of having to tip-toe around you all the time.

Dealing treacherously with your spouse can lead to divorce, and God hates divorce. Malachi 2:16 says, "For the Lord God of Israel says that He hates divorce, for it covers one's garment with violence. So guard yourselves; always remain loyal to your wife."

The last verse of this chapter talks about *evil people **seemingly** getting away with evil.* Corruption is happening around them, the evildoers are not punished, and the Israelites are in essence nagging God, saying, "Where is the God of justice?"

There is a time for God's patience, and there is also a time for judgement. We read in 2 Peter 3:9–10, "The Lord is not slow in keeping his promise, as some understand slowness. He is patient with you, not wanting anyone to perish, but everyone to come to repentance. But the day of the Lord will come like a thief. The heavens will disappear with a roar; the elements will be destroyed by fire, and the earth and everything in it will be laid bare." Those unrepentant of their evil will be judged—here on earth and for eternity in hell. I wish this eternal punishment on no one. Lord, work in every heart!

Chapter 3

God responds to these accusations in verse 17 with, "Behold, I send my messenger, and he will prepare the way before me." God gives a warning to His church, and instructions to change or turn from its ways; "And the Lord, whom you seek, will suddenly come to His temple." His appearance will be powerful! His appearance is described to be *like a refiner's fire* and *like launderer's soap.* I believe *His appearance* is the Holy Spirit showing up strong and mighty, in full force!

What is the purpose of a refining fire? To remove impurities. "The Bible often uses the imagery of gold being refined as a picture of what God does in our lives…. He is the refiner and we are the lump of unrefined gold, full of impurity and full of potential beauty" (www.mrt.com). God *allows* the fire or trials in our lives—not to destroy us, but to remove the impurities and sin we so desperately must be rid of. We are saved by the blood, but we must let go of the baggage (sin). No impure thing will enter the kingdom of God. Even in the fire, God is showing how merciful and loving He is, not wanting for anyone to perish in eternal damnation, but to be cleansed and purified.

What is launderer's soap used for? From science class, I remember learning about the role of soap; "Soap is an excellent cleanser because of its ability to act as an emulsifying agent. An emulsifier is capable of dispersing one liquid into another immiscible liquid. This means that while oil (which attracts dirt) doesn't naturally mix with water, soap can suspend oil/dirt in such a way that it can be removed" (thoughtco.com).

It appears that the *launderer's soap* breaks an unseen chain—the chain of sin. One of the roles of the Holy Spirit (oil) is to convict the world of sin (dirt and filth) (John 16:8). Once a person is convicted, he or she can repent. One source explains, "Repentance is indeed able to break the chain of sin and to lead man out of the cycle of passions and vices" (blog.obitel-minsk. com).

Even in the Old Testament, we find a correspondence between the Holy Spirit and the dismantling of sin. The anointing (pouring of oil) breaks the yoke (sin and bondage), setting captives free (Isaiah 10:27). Unfortunately, sin exists in every human heart and must come out. The oil, or the Holy Spirit, lives and speaks through believers walking in truth, who are filled with the Spirit. Once truth is revealed to me and to you— repent! Don't wait, for this is your moment of salvation.

God comes to purify, purge, cleanse, and restore—not to kill. Once the church is purified, it can offer a pleasing offering, "an offering in righteousness." God will then swiftly judge sorcerers, adulterers, perjurers, and other evil people who do not fear God.

Next, He says to the Israelites, "You have gone away from my ordinances and have not kept them. Return to me, and I will return to you." Who acts first? Man does. God wants His people to return to the obedience of His Word. How else can we return to God? By returning to our first love—by doing those acts we did *at first.*

Here in Malachi 3:8–12, God describes *returning to Him* as tithing to the storehouse, and giving offerings. God promises blessings in abundance, in exchange for obedience in the area of tithing on *all* of your profits (income and increases), to the storehouse (the church body that you attend regularly or consider yourself to be a part of). Offerings should be given also, however, in my understanding, offerings can be given to whomever you feel led by the Holy Spirit to give to (a brother, a friend, a homeless person, etc.). But the full tithe must be given to the storehouse, God's house where you worship (see also My house will be called a house of prayer; Matthew 21:13).

If we obey this principle wholly, God will also *rebuke the devourer on our behalf.* What does this mean? It means He will give us financial wisdom—teaching us how to save and preserve what we have worked hard for (not just spend money frivolously), and training us to make wise investments in all of our family expenses (food, clothing, car and home insurance, interest rates for loans, stock investments, etc.).

If we do not obey God in the area of tithes and offerings, this is a serious offense, with a curse attached: "Will man rob God? Yet you are robbing me. But you say, 'How have we robbed you?' In your tithes and contributions. You are cursed with a curse, for you are robbing me, the whole nation of you" (verses 8–9).

If you have ever stepped into a church, you have heard of giving the tithe, ten percent of your income. Giving the tithe is biblical. You give God 10% and *keep 90%*; not a bad deal. The tithe is used to pay for the Lord's workers: senior pastor, support pastors, youth leaders, children's church pastors, family counselors, prayer partners, and other staff in the ministry. Most assuredly, this scripture wasn't meant to be abused by church pastors or leadership—getting extremely wealthy off of the tithe—instead of using finances appropriately, for the needs of the kingdom of God. Remember, Jesus overturned the tables of the money changers in the temple, and said, "My house will be called a house of prayer, but you are making it a den of robbers" (Matthew 21:13).

Many churches in America understand this scripture, are aware of the needs today, and have paid staff to meet the people's needs. However, not all churches follow this practice. "Bring the whole tithe into the storehouse, *that there may be food in my house."* If we obey this scripture, there will be food in His house. We can deduct that *if we do not obey this scripture, there will not be food in His house.*

What kind of food? In the Lord's prayer, we pray, "Give us this day our daily bread." Also in the gospels, Jesus says to the devil, "Man will not live by bread alone, but by every word that proceeds out of the mouth of God." Based on these scriptures, *the food* is both earthly and spiritual food. Earthly food will help those in need—instead of the poor having to rely on the government. But, how do you feed someone spiritually? By teaching him or her the Word of God.

The tithe provides financial support, to supply a spiritual mission. When you have a full-time paid pastor and church staff, that's what they do. A church staffer's first priority is their job at church—not working a nine-to-five job and volunteering evenings and weekends to pastor a church (for example). Getting burnt out, and neglecting your family in the process of service to God, *is not* part of God's plan. God's plan is that the staff's *first fruits* or the prime hours of the day when a person has the best to offer, the most energy—would be spent doing the Lord's work. Then the church will be equipped or have food to offer those who are lost and hurting, as well as food for its members.

There are so many struggles people face today—people are hurting (inside and outside of the church). The Church of Christ should be where people can find salvation, support, and solutions. If the world flooded our churches today, could we even handle it? We need to get equipped.

God says, "Put me to the test." He challenges us—today—to be obedient with all of our earnings. If we obey God in giving tithes and offerings, He will "throw open the floodgates of heaven and pour out so much blessing that there will not be room enough to store it." Blessings will flow automatically. You don't have to "name it and claim it" nor command it to come. *God* commands a blessing over His people, when they walk in love, unity, and obedience to His Word (see Psalm 133).

Moving forward in Malachi 3, we see in verse 13, that God recognizes the harsh words of some of the people, saying it is useless to serve God and keep His ordinances; "Those who do wickedness are raised up; they even tempt God and go free." They are seeing through human eyes, that the evil are getting away with murder for example; however, we are called to have spiritual eyes. Spiritual eyes tell us that God is just, and that God is never late. God is always working; He never stops working, in the realm of the seen and unseen.

These Israelites do not have *the fear of the Lord*— they speak to God with irreverence. However, what happens next is a beautiful thing; "Then those who feared the Lord spoke with each other, and the Lord listened to what they said. And a book of remembrance was written before Him, for those who fear the Lord and meditate on His name."

What captured God's attention? Irreverance, complaining, and disobedience? No. What grabbed God's attention, and prompted a book of remembrance to be written, was *the conversations of those who fear Him and meditate on His name.* God says specifically of these people, "They shall be mine... On the day I make them My jewels. And I will spare them..." Spare them from what? Perhaps sickness, disease, disasters on the earth—such as those that describe the last days in the Bible. I'm not sure. Either way, I desire to be in the group that is spared, and that group is *the group that fears God and meditates on His name daily.*

Chapter 3 concludes with *discernment coming back to the people.* They will again be able to discern between one who serves God (the righteous) and one who does not serve Him (the wicked). This element is critical. In a world full of lies and deception (outside and inside of the church), discernment—*the ability to judge well*—is needed like never before.

Chapter 4

This last chapter of Malachi talks about the coming day of judgement for all who do wicked things—they will be burnt up—but the righteous will be victorious; "But for those who fear the Lord, the Sun of Righteousness shall arise with healing in His wings...they that fear the Lord will go free...and trample the wicked as if they were dust under your feet, on that day." Furthermore, God says to *remember* and *obey* the Law of Moses, the Ten Commandments.

Before the day of the Lord arrives, God says He will first send the prophet Elijah, who will preach, and turn the hearts of parents to their children, and the hearts of children to their parents. There are different opinions on this—which Elijah is being referenced here?

If we look forward 400 years, to the coming of John the Baptist, Jesus speaks in the book of Matthew of John the Baptist; "As they went away, Jesus began to speak to the crowds concerning John: "What did you go out into the wilderness to see? A reed shaken by the wind? What then did you go out to see? A man dressed in soft clothing? Behold, those who wear soft clothing are in kings' houses. What then did you go out to see? A prophet? Yes, I tell you, and more than a prophet. This is he of whom it is written, 'Behold, I send my messenger before your face, who will prepare your way before you.' Truly, I say to you, among those born of women there has arisen no one greater than John the Baptist. Yet the one who is least in the kingdom of heaven is greater than he. From the days of John the Baptist until now the kingdom of heaven has suffered violence, and the violent take it by force. For all the Prophets and the Law prophesied until John, and if you are willing to accept it, he is Elijah who is to come. He who has ears to hear, let him hear" (Matthew 11: 7–15).

We know that John the Baptist came, preparing the way of the Lord, during the time when Jesus was on earth. Likewise, in our time, the Spirit of God is working and preparing the way for the Lord's return on the clouds—to take God's children with Him for eternity!

Let us be filled with the Holy Spirit, and be known as a praying people. May we fear God, meditate daily on His name, and be obedient to His Word. Let us be faithful to God and to our marriages, and repent and be purified of sin—where we have fallen short. In everything we do, may we always offer the Lord our best!

Chapter 12

We Are in a War

Did you know that you are in a war? Once you receive Christ in your heart, you pass from spiritual death to life. The spiritual realm, some say, is more real than the world we see now with our earthly eyes. In the spiritual realm, there is the Holy Spirit and the angels *and* the devil and his demons. The Bible says in Ephesians 6:20, "For we do not wrestle against flesh and blood, but against principalities, against powers, against the rulers of the darkness of this age, against spiritual hosts of wickedness in the heavenly places." You are not at war with other Christians, or even other people that are unsaved. You are at war with the devil and the forces of darkness. The sooner we realize this truth, the better.

Not a day goes by that we don't hear about this tragedy or that virus, homelessness, dishonesty in politics, promises made and then ignored, or hunger and poverty—not only in third world countries but in America also. Some parents are addicted to drugs, alcohol, social media, gambling, or pornography; as a result, families (children and parents) are suffering. Adults, as well as children, are suffering from depression, anxiety, and panic attacks. Since God is good and no evil exists in Him, there is only one that is responsible for all this evil—the devil.

Apostle Peter, *the rock*, warns us; "Be sober, be vigilant; because your adversary the devil walks about like a roaring lion, seeking whom he may devour. Resist him, steadfast in the faith, knowing that the same sufferings are experienced by your brotherhood in the world" (1 Peter 5:8–9). He is *like* a roaring lion, seeking whom he can devour. He is not a lion, rather he gives the perception of being a lion.

One day as I was driving with my kids, my boys were having a debate in the backseat. My younger son was saying that the devil is big and powerful and that he was going to get power from him. My older son was fighting back, and rebuking him at the same time, saying that the devil is weak, and God is the strongest of anyone. The truth is, in size and strength, the devil has the likeness of a vermin, a rodent—small and weak, pretending to be powerful like a lion. Some people, even Christians, believe the devil is powerful. Not true! The Bible says, "Greater is He that is in me, than he that is in the world." What you believe is important, and it is important to know that the devil is weak, only pretending to be strong.

The devil roams the earth and circles the heavens for now (gotquestions.org). The appointed time is coming when the devil will be destroyed in the lake of fire (Revelation 20:10). More than once, my sons have asked why the devil isn't bound up and cast into the lake of fire, yet. It's a good question. I believe it is for the testing of our faith *and* the testing of our love. If these remain untested, how does one know if their faith and love are authentic and true? Furthermore, God is a God of free will. Man chooses whom he will follow—God or Satan. Only two options exist. Choosing one negates the other (Matthew 6:24), and choosing neither by default places you at enmity with God, therefore a member of Satan's team (Revelation 3:16).

The devil is only as powerful as man allows him to be, as he works through people walking in disobedience and also through his demons (who can reside in people and must be cast out). Remember, Jesus forgave sins, healed the sick, and cast out demons—almost simultaneously. When a person walks in disobedience to any of the laws of God, this *rebellion* acts like a tool of the devil and a person *naively* carries out the plans of the devil. Ephesians 2:1–3 says, "And you He made alive, who were dead in trespasses and sins, in which you once walked according to the course of this world, according to the prince of the power of the air, the spirit who now works in

262

the sons of disobedience, among whom also we all once conducted ourselves in the lusts of our flesh, fulfilling the desires of the flesh and of the mind, and were by nature children of wrath, just as the others." We are *all* guilty of this. However, walking in obedience to all of God's Word makes us a tool of righteousness in *God's hands*.

In some cases, people actually choose to serve the devil and are Satan worshippers. Some Hollywood stars, wealthy politicians, and others in high positions in this world have given themselves to Satan. Of course this never makes the news but it is real. Stars invite the devil to inhabit them and are used as instruments of evil—attracting your kids to listen, to attend concerts, to partake in a demonic environment.

Fear

The devil is real, the devil is weak, and the devil is also a liar. He uses fear through lies to control people and keep them down. We all have experienced and will experience fear. We must learn the truth about fear. Lies exposed with truth dissolves fear or *disarms fear*.

If we have fear, it didn't come from God—for fear is an attribute of the devil; "For God has not give us a spirit of fear, but of power and of love and of a sound mind" (2 Timothy 1:7). When we are fearful, anxious, and worried, we must recognize these as a foreign enemy. These *are not* attributes of the Holy Spirit.

Fear must be resisted; "Submit yourselves therefore to God. Resist the devil, and he will flee from you" (James 4:7). What does it mean to resist something? To withstand, strive against, or oppose (dictionary.com). When something is resisted, it cannot penetrate to the other side. Once you have done your part, *resist the devil*, he flees. He must flee, for God's Word says so. Believe and apply God's Word and you will be victorious over fear *every time*.

Fortunately, I have learned to detect fear. When I find myself worried or anxious, my heart rate up, I know it's time to resist the devil. This may sound funny if you are not used to this type of thinking. However, you must fight the devil and fear with the truths found in God's Word, by faith that God's Word has power. I have had to do this many times, and it works. It might be as simple as realizing that you are fearing and that no real threat exists. Oftentimes, once I realize this, peace takes over.

Furthermore, fear may exist in your heart. Personally, some of my first memories included fear. I carried fear in my heart for many years, not because I wanted to, but because I thought it was somehow normal. *Fear must be cast out*. If you don't cast it out, you will suffer, and you do not have to suffer. We read in

1 John 4:18 about perfect love; "There is no fear in love, but perfect love casts out fear. For fear has to do with punishment, and whoever fears has not been perfected in love." We have the love of Christ in us; however, it must be perfected by the help of the Holy Spirit. Perfected love is power —power to heal in Jesus' name, power to save in Jesus' name, and power to cast out anything that is not of God—in Jesus' name. After fear is cast out of your heart, instantly peace floods in, and you can continue with the Spirit of power and of a sound mind.

By the Holy Spirit, God has given us a *sound mind*—a peaceful mind, free of the lies of the devil. In order to experience peace in your life every day, even in the storm, you must be filled with God's Spirit—the Spirit of truth. The more time we spend with the Holy Spirit, the stronger we become in the Spirit, learning to discern truth from lies—and cast out lies that enter our minds. We can fight every spiritual battle and win, in Jesus' name!

Dear brother and dear sister, you are the righteousness of God in Christ Jesus! God says, rise up and take your place at the table! The battle has been won by Jesus on the cross. The same Spirit that dwells in Jesus, raising Him from the dead, dwells in us who believe. That is truth and amazing news! Don't allow the devil—through your emotions, circumstances, or people—to tell you otherwise. When the devil comes, and he will, you can kick him back to the pit where he belongs, by speaking words of truth from God's Word. He must flee!

In my former job as a pharmaceutical sales representative, I learned about mental illness and mood disorders. I believe these exist. However, it is critical to discern what you are faced with. Is this a spiritual attack (from the devil) or depression? The Holy Spirit, the Spirit of truth, can and will lead you to know the difference. You must know what you are up against so you can take the next appropriate step. If it is an attack from the devil, resist him and he must flee. If it is sickness, partnering with a faith-filled friend, family member, or pastor is biblical—and will bring you victory. James 5:16 says, "Therefore confess your sins to each other and pray for each other so that you may be healed. The prayer of a righteous person is powerful and effective."

It is not very popular to confess your sins to someone. However, the Bible is telling us this is a prerequisite for receiving healing. Just like lies exposed with truth dissolves fear or disarms fear, *sin exposed disarms sin*. Find a mature Christian you can trust to confess your sins to, and pray together for physical, mental, emotional, and spiritual healing.

I personally am not anti-medication. I believe taking medication should be *temporary*, not a lifelong solution. In fact, doctors tell their patients with high blood pressure, diabetes, obesity, etc., to make lifestyle changes; and if they would, most diseases would disappear. What usually happens, is that patients do not make lifestyle changes. As a result, they remain on medications—sometimes twelve medications or more—for decades (the rest of their life). We must change our diet and exercise routine, in order to be healthy and to properly fight diseases.

I believe the same about mood disorder medications—*they should be temporary*. While on medication, take the time to consult a Christian counselor or therapist, to get to the root of your problem, instead of continuing to place a Band-Aid on it with medication.

I read what one of my junior high friends wrote on Facebook, following two years of taking anti-anxiety medication. To sum it up, the medication helped suppress the anxiety and panic attacks. However, it also suppressed her overall emotions— emotions of joy, enthusiasm for life, and it also suppressed feeling God's presence. God gave us *emotions* to connect with Him, to connect with one another, to feel alive. He gave emotions to men and women; this is a good thing. You don't want to be ruled by emotions, but ignoring or suppressing emotions will cripple you. Emotion is from God and should be embraced, considered, and not ignored.

So once my friend began to reduce her dose, in efforts to get off the medication completely, she began to feel God again and feel alive again. This is something to consider if you find yourself battling with mental or emotional struggles, and are considering or currently taking any sort of mood disorder medication. Medication will help with your lows or highs, but it will also place a fog between you and God, *and* between you and others. As we know, it is difficult to see through the fog.

The good news is, there is power, above all evil and disease, in the name of Jesus! This power is for *all believers*; "And these signs will accompany those who believe: In my name they will drive out demons; they will speak in new tongues; they will pick up snakes with their hands; and when they drink deadly poison, it will not hurt them at all; they will place their hands on sick people, and they will get well" (Mark 16:17–18).

When Jesus paid the price on the cross for our sins, He also paid the price for us to have peace and be healed of all sickness and disease; "But He was wounded for our transgressions, He was bruised for our iniquities; the chastisement for our peace was upon Him, And by His stripes we are healed" (Isaiah 53:5).

The devil wants you weak with disease so he can control you through isolation, medication, and depression—until you finally die. God wants you strong, healthy, and healed so you can overcome the attacks of the devil and live in freedom, joy, and peace. The devil wants you to sin, putting you in a compromised state, where even a mediocre blow could destroy you. God wants you to resist sin and turn to Him always, and in Him you will find rest and be fulfilled.

Weapons

We learned at the beginning of this chapter that we in fact are wrestling against the unseen spiritual realm—the realm of darkness. In order to fight this evil, we need spiritual gear, for "the weapons of our warfare are not carnal." The weapons of a Christian's warfare are spiritual. Thankfully, in God's kingdom there are *weapons*, and the only way we will survive this spiritual battle is by "putting on the full armor of God," which is a spiritual armor.

What kind of armor does the Christian have at his or her disposal? Ephesians 6 describes this godly armor; "Therefore take up the whole armor of God, that you may be able to withstand in the evil day, and having done all, to stand firm. Stand therefore, having fastened on the belt of truth, and having put on the breastplate of righteousness, and, as shoes for your feet, having put on the readiness given by the gospel of peace. In all circumstances take up the shield of faith, with which you can extinguish all the flaming darts of the evil one; and take the helmet of salvation, and the sword of the Spirit, which is the Word of God." Notice all the *action words* in this scripture: take up, withstand, stand firm, stand, fasten, put on, and readiness. *The armor does not just land on you.* You must act and put it on. Whether you have the armor on or not depends on you, not on God. The armor is yours for the taking. You want to get equipped, because you want to be successful. You don't want to be scratching your head wondering why this Christian thing isn't working *or* worse yet, blame God because this Christian thing isn't working.

The belt of truth usually occurs first. When men prepared for battle, the belt (with strips of leather and metal hanging down from it) was the first piece of armor Roman soldiers put on, protecting some of the most vital organs and arteries. Similarly, putting on the spiritual belt is a critical first step in getting equipped for a spiritual battle. Once you know the truth (Jesus is the Holy Son of God, Jesus came in the flesh, Jesus loved you so much that He died for you and rose again), you can accept Jesus as Lord and Savior. By reading the Bible, and through the filling of the Holy Spirit, God will continue to reveal truth to you—daily. You are ready for the next armor, *the helmet of salvation;* "Because, if you confess with your mouth that Jesus is Lord and believe in your heart that God raised Him from the dead, you will be saved" (Romans 10:9).

270

When you receive Jesus, you receive righteousness, if you remain in Christ, if you abide in Him or *obey* God's Word (2 Corinthians 5:21). When we choose to live uprightly, we are putting on *the breastplate of righteousness*. The breastplate covers some of the most important parts of the body (heart, lungs, etc), and is critical in preserving a soldier's life when in battle. Likewise, when we obey God's Word, when we choose to walk uprightly, our spiritual life will be preserved as *holy*.

After I got saved, I made a public confession of my new life by getting baptized in water. I also started to read the Bible every day, *the sword of the Spirit*. You must read the manual or Bible. It doesn't make you *more saved,* rather it equips you. In order for the Bible to be a sword in your life, you must believe; you must obey and apply what you have read—daily.

The shield of faith will also arise the more you read your Bible and fill your heart and mind with truth. The shield of faith blocks against the attacks of the devil on your mind. The devil comes with thoughts of doubt and fear, while the Holy Spirit and Bible sow seeds of faith in our minds and hearts.

As shoes for your feet, having put on the readiness given by the gospel of peace. The *readiness* reminds me of my track days—waiting in the markers, in position, ready for the race to start. Christians should be ready at all times to be the hands and feet of Jesus—day or night—equipped with the gospel of peace.

271

Additionally, our feet are to search for peace and chase after it; "Keep your tongue from evil and your lips from deceitful speech. Turn away from evil and do good; *seek peace and pursue it*. The eyes of the LORD are on the righteous, and His ears are inclined to their cry" (Psalm 34:13–15).

Walking in truth and having true peace is not just putting up with stuff because you want to avoid conflict, avoid rejection, or avoid hurting someone's feelings. Loving people includes telling them the truth, in love. The *love* part can be difficult to grasp, especially if we get into a heated topic. I am guilty of this and must remember to speak in love, above all, and maintain peace while speaking truth. If we are obedient to the truths God reveals to us, He will reveal even more truth. In essence, we graduate or move from glory to glory.

Every Christian must equip themselves with *the full armor of God:* the belt of truth, the helmet of salvation, the sword of the spirit, the breastplate of righteousness, the shield of faith, and the shoes of the gospel of peace. Keep in mind this is not a list of do's, but rather the right way to equip yourself for living a successful Christian life. By success I mean enjoying everything God has for you and your family, while making disciples everywhere you go. We make disciples by changing the way people think. We can impact our children, our spouses, our families, our friends, and co-workers—for God's kingdom. Whatever mission field God gave you—work the field for His glory. Remember, the enemy is real and is easily defeated. However, we must be aware of his schemes, be equipped, and fight back the right way.

Discernment

Another way we fight against the powers of darkness is by having our sensibilities sharpened, having discernment. The Bible says in Hebrews, "For everyone who lives on milk is still an infant, inexperienced in the message of righteousness. But solid food is for the mature, who by constant use have trained their sensibilities to distinguish good from evil" (Hebrews 5:13–14). What are sensibilities? "Sensibility is the ability to receive sensations; awareness of and responsiveness toward something (such as emotion in another); susceptibility to a pleasurable or painful impression; sensitiveness" (www.merriam-webster.com). Furthermore, one online source said, "In its simplest definition, discernment is nothing more than the ability to decide between truth and error, right and wrong. Discernment is the process of making careful distinctions in our thinking about truth" (www.terigyemi.com).

With training and patience, you will be able to discern lies from truth. This is the product of partnering with the Holy Spirit. If you just react, like what I did for too many years, you can, and I did, make many mistakes in discerning a situation.

Has there ever been such a critical time as this for truth? People make a lifestyle out of lying and don't think twice about it. Lives are destroyed and even lost as a result. Truth is needed like never before! That is why you must take this scripture to heart, and train your sensibilities, with the help of the Holy Spirit.

How will we know if a pastor is authentic, or if a worship group or certain songs are godly? Even regarding local and world events, how can we know who is telling us the truth and who is tricking us with lies? We will know by the Holy Spirit or the *Spirit of Truth*. Always keep in mind that the devil is on the side of destruction, corruption, lies, poverty, sickness, sin, chaos, control, and death. That is all devil. God represents first of all truth— then love, joy, peace, life, light, freedom, unity around truth, forgiveness, restoration, justice, abundant health,and multiplication (including bearing children). Anything good and pure is of God.

Most often, the first things we perceive with our earthly senses—sight, hearing, or even our feelings—are misleading. We must dig deeper. Even fresh water is not found at the surface, but lies much deeper below the surface. Likewise, truth lies below the surface. We must use our *spiritual senses*. Do not rush for answers. Wait. Wait on the Lord. That's why patience is so important and must be learned from childhood. We wait on the Lord, not panic and race to and fro. Wait. Your waiting will produce answers—true answers. This is what the Lord taught me over time.

Once you've trained your senses, once you've moved from milk to meat, God can share insight with you by the Holy Spirit. If the Lord shows you that a pastor is, let's say, after your money, He is showing you for a reason. That reason is not to run around spreading the news to whomever will listen. First, pray for that person. Next, you and I have a responsibility to share truth in love with the person we believe is not walking in truth. This must be clear in scripture, meaning clearly defined as sin, not just personal opinion or tradition that they are breaking. If the person does not want to hear what you have to say, I believe it is biblical to involve a mature Christian leader of the matter. After that, you are released from your responsibility and can rest easy. God will reward you for sharing truth. Remember, we are Christ's representatives on this planet and have a responsibility to *share the truth in love* (Ephesians 4:25), with the motive of the heart being restoration.

Apostle Peter once wisely said, "Above all, keep loving one another earnestly, since love covers a multitude of sins" (1 Peter 4:8). Where did we get the idea that once we see flaws or sin in someone, we should abandon them and throw them to the wolves? Love does not throw someone to the wolves— *love covers*. Bear in mind, we are all flawed, "For all have sinned and fall short of the glory of God, and all are justified freely by his grace through the redemption that came by Christ Jesus" (Romans 3:23–24). Love prays, love fasts, love intercedes and shares truth with other believers. Remember, Christ is our example, and we should desire what He desires; "The Lord is not slow to fulfill his promise as some count slowness, but is patient toward you, not wishing that any should perish, but that all should reach repentance" (2 Peter 3:9).

To truly live a successful Christian life, we cannot live and die by what we experience with our human senses and human thinking. The Bible says, "Trust in the LORD with all your heart, and do not lean on your own understanding. In all your ways acknowledge him, and he shall direct your paths" (Proverbs 3:5). A human's understanding is limited. We only see in part, while God sees everything. But when we are fully surrendered and committed to Jesus, and filled with the Holy Spirit—not our understanding—but the Holy Spirit is guiding and leading us.

We know we are full of the Holy Spirit when we are exemplifying the fruit of the Spirit: love, joy, peace, patience, kindness, goodness, faithfulness, gentleness, and self-control. When we are living in love, self-control, etc., the Holy Spirit is able to communicate with us *ahead of time*. He informs us of the plans and schemes of the devil. The Holy Spirit also illuminates us of God's plan of salvation, restoration, and blessings for individuals —so we can take action. Often times, *taking action* is praying and interceding. Other times, we have to tell someone or ourselves, some truth. Whatever the situation, the Holy Spirit will lead us. We can rest in this.

As we wrap up these twelve chapters, and if you haven't already done so—take these action items to heart, and put them into practice by the grace of God:

- ❖ Be saved, you and your household, through Jesus Christ
- ❖ Be water baptized, as evidence of your decision
- ❖ Be baptized with the Holy Spirit, by the laying on of hands of your pastor
- ❖ Communicate with God—pray all the time, even in your mind
- ❖ Fast & pray on a regular basis
- ❖ Show God love—read your Bible every day and obey it's words
- ❖ Show your neighbor love—through actions, loving others as you love yourself
- ❖ Find a Christian church, a family, to be a part of consistently

These action items are voluntary, and God forces no one—although He encourages us and advises all to come to Him and receive eternal life. Hell is real. Heaven is real. Beloved, choose Jesus Christ today and be a citizen of heaven for eternity!

Jesus went to prepare a marvelous place for His children and will return soon; "But, as it is written, 'What no eye has seen, nor ear heard, nor the heart of man imagined, what God has prepared for those who love him'" (1 Corinthians 2:9). However, before Jesus returns, crooked paths must be straightened out, making a straight road for the Lord. Truth is a straight road. Truth from God's Word must reach every human, to the ends of the earth, then the end will come (Matthew 24:14). While we joyfully wait for Jesus to return on the clouds, "The Spirit and the bride say, "Come!" And let the one who hears say, "Come!" Let the one who is thirsty come; and let the one who wishes take the free gift of the water of life" (Revelation 22:17). Come, Lord Jesus!

About the Author

Tabitha Sabou is a Christian author—producing both children's books and captivating biblically-based books for all readers. She was born into a Romanian Christian family in the Detroit, Michigan area. Currently she lives in the same area—along with her husband of over twenty years, two young sons, two young daughters, and newborn son. Tabitha also belongs to the same church she grew up in since childhood (a conservative Romanian-speaking

Pentecostal church). Tabitha feels blessed to be an American-Romanian, living in this great Christian-founded nation, yet having been raised in an almost alternate dimension within the Romanian culture—with Romanian foods, Romanian slang, and Romanian Christianity (very different from American Christianity). Taking the best from both cultures has helped her understand *the love of God* and *the fear of the Lord.* Tabitha's desire, since childhood, is to help others. Through her heart-felt words written in books, she can now help many people, even people around the globe, for the glory of God. *To connect with Tabitha, or invite her to speak at your church or event, please send an email to tabitha.author@yahoo.com.*

Made in the USA
Columbia, SC
01 July 2025

60195149R00159